Creative Ways to Build
Christian Community

The House of Prisca and Aquila

OUR MISSION AT THE House of Prisca and Aquila is to produce quality books that expound accurately the word of God to empower women and men to minister together in a multicultural church. Our writers have a positive view of the Bible as God's revelation that affects both thoughts and words, so it is plenary, historically accurate, and consistent in itself, fully reliable, and authoritative as God's revelation. Because God is true, God's revelation is true, inclusive to men and women and speaking to a multicultural church, wherein all the diversity of the church is represented within the parameters of egalitarianism and inerrancy.

The word of God is what we are expounding, thereby empowering women and men to minister together in all levels of the church and home. The reason we say women and men together is because that is the model of Prisca and Aquila, ministering together to another member of the church—Apollos: "Having heard Apollos, Priscilla and Aquila took him aside and more accurately expounded to him the Way of God" (Acts 18:26). True exposition, like true religion, is by no means boring—it is fascinating. Books that reveal and expound God's true nature "burn within us" as they elucidate the Scripture and apply it to our lives.

This was the experience of the disciples who heard Jesus on the road to Emmaus: "Were not our hearts burning while Jesus was talking to us on the road, while he was opening the scriptures to us?" (Luke 24:32). We are hoping to create the classics of tomorrow, significant and accessible trade and academic books that "burn within us."

Our "house" is like the home to which Prisca and Aquila no doubt brought Apollos as they took him aside. It is like the home in Emmaus where Jesus stopped to break bread and reveal his presence. It is like the house built on the rock of obedience to Jesus (Matt 7:24). Our "house," as a euphemism for our publishing team, is a home where truth is shared and Jesus' Spirit breaks bread with us, nourishing all of us with his bounty of truth.

We are delighted to work together with Wipf and Stock in this series and welcome submissions on a wide variety of topics from an egalitarian, inerrantist global perspective.

For more information, see our website: sites.google.com/site/houseofpriscaandaquila/.

Creative Ways to Build Christian Community

EDITED BY
JEANNE C. DEFAZIO
JOHN P. LATHROP

Preface by William David Spencer

WIPF & STOCK · Eugene, Oregon

CREATIVE WAYS TO BUILD CHRISTIAN COMMUNITY

Copyright © 2013 by Jeanne DeFazio and John P. Lathrop. All rights reserved. Except for brief quotations in critical publications or reviews, no part of this book may be reproduced in any manner without prior written permission from the publisher. Write: Permissions, Wipf & Stock Publishers, 199 W. 8th Ave., Suite 3, Eugene, OR 07401.

Wipf & Stock
An Imprint of Wipf & Stock Publishers
199 W. 8th Ave., Suite 3
Eugene, OR 97401
www.wipfandstock.com.

ISBN 13: 978-1-62032-745-6

Manufactured in the U.S.A.

Scripture quotations marked NIV are taken from the Holy Bible, New International Version,*NIV.* Copyright © 1973, 1978, 1984, 2011 by Biblica, Inc. Used by permission of Zondervan. All rights reserved. www.zondervan.com.

Scripture quotations marked NASB are taken from the New American Standard Bible*, Copyright © 1960, 1962, 1963, 1968, 1971, 1972, 1973, 1975, 1977, 1995 by The Lockman Foundation. Used with permission.

Scripture references identified KJV are taken from the King James Version of the Bible.

This book is dedicated to all those who feel God tugging at their heartstrings to serve him. If you are feeling unworthy to serve God, you are not alone. My youth was spent in the time and state of "California Dreamin."[1] By personal experience I am an unlikely candidate to graduate from or to teach in a seminary. I was inspired and motivated to do so by the example of Jerry Brown, a former seminarian and the current Governor of the State of California.

JEANNE DEFAZIO

---

1. Phillips, "California Dreamin,'" 1978.

Contents

Preface by William David Spencer ix
Acknowledgements xvii
Introduction xix

1
Building Christian Community
Through Meetings and Meals 1
Jeanne DeFazio

2
Agape Feasts 27
Teresa Flowers

3
The Arts:
An Essential Dialogue for the Body of Christ 38
Olga Soler

4
A Listening Heart 56
Cathy Squires

5
A Look at New Beginnings 66
Jeff Marks

6
Summing It Up 79
Olga Soler

Contributors 85
Bibliography 89

Preface

WHEN A 27-YEAR-OLD MAN from Tokyo fell in love with and subsequently married an animated character from Nintendo's *Love Plus* video game, we might have expected his bereaved parents or concerned employer or landlady to have called for an ambulance with white-coated paramedics waving straightjackets. But nothing of the sort took place. Instead, he hosted a full-scale celebration before "a priest, an MC, a DJ" with "photo slideshows, wedding music and even a bouquet." Instead of a week in a medical facility for observation, he went on a honeymoon. As he explained, "I love this character, not a machine. . .I understand 100 percent that this is a game. I understand very well that I cannot marry her physically or legally." Yet, he found this virtual character "better than a human girlfriend."[1] "Some people have expressed doubts about my actions, but at the end of the day, this is really just about us as husband and wife. As long as the two of us can go on to create a happy household, I'm sure any misgivings about us will be resolved."[2] This rational young man has become a living example of what internet-addiction expert Hiroshi Ashizake has observed, "Today's Japanese youth can't express their true feelings in reality. They can only do it in the virtual world."[3] But, this malady is not limited to Japan. Nor is it an action without a fall-out effect on someone (and not just

---

1. Kyung Lah, "Tokyo Man," CNN.com.
2. Nicole Navarro, "Man Marries," indieregister.com.
3. Kyung Lah, "Tokyo Man," CNN.com.

Preface

the draw pile of eligible young boys available for hopeful girls of this island nation). The victim here is community.

In recent articles in *Africanus Journal*, I have been speculating on the nature of personhood, marriage, and interpersonal relations in a future increasingly shaped by artificial intelligence, especially focused in android robotics (simulating human partners in malebots and fembots), as well as disembodied virtual relationships (through the increasing transference of identity into virtual avatars who interact in simulated environments like internet "chat rooms," video games, and meta-verses). The fall out has been the increasing number of real-life divorces naming as the alienating culprit a virtual partner, met, perhaps, in a special interest chat room, or in the elaborate, animated virtual meta-nation, Second Life.[4] The irony is that the offending virtual adulterers may never actually meet in real life, yet the intimate bond of marriage with their spouses in the real world has been supplanted and shattered as irreparably as if they had sneaked off to some sleazy motel with rooms by the hour.

How did we arrive at such a present state of human engagement? Why are we confronting such a future threat to interpersonal relationships? And what on earth can we do about these situations now, before they are epidemic across the globe?

Technology has brought us many blessings, all built on the expansion of communication. Data that once

---

4. Those who would like to know more of my thoughts on these developments may consult the free on-line *Africanus Journal* at http://www.gordonconwell.edu/boston/africanusjournal for my two articles, "Should the *Imago Dei* Be Extended to Robots? *Love and Sex with Robots,* the Future of Marriage, and the Christian Concept of Personhood" (Vol. 1, No. 2 [November 2009] 6–19), and "Cyber Marriage, Virtual Adultery, Real Consequences, and the Need for a Techno Sexual Ethic" (Vol. 2, No. 2 [November 2010] 14–22).

Preface

seemed nearly insurmountably impossible to ferret out of unfathomable archives are now simply a right question and a double click away. Keepsakes and memorabilia we thought lost irretrievably in the shadowy memories of our past are now displayed on eBay with prices driven down by competition—sometimes cheaper to buy now than we remember they cost then. Whole virtual communities are built out of interest groups that are global in expanse. The internet is all about networking. But the irony is that at the same time it can be isolating.

Let me share one small, but, to me, significant example. Years ago, I could pass a sign-up sheet around my classroom and have everyone write down their contact information to add to my roll book. For the last twenty years, despite my pleas, my students have become incapable of passing such a sheet to one another, so that it goes all the way around the room. This seems like such a minor annoyance, it is hardly worth noticing. I think differently. I believe it is telling me something very serious about their personal skills. I may be training them in what to many may appear to be an abstract discipline, theology, but the point of this topic, as in all their training, is to help them become fully equipped pastors, counselors, and lay leaders, who can minister to a congregation, a para-church organization, a client base, a classroom.

What I am perceiving is that they are so used to being at their desks or computer consoles, in their cubicles, working on their laptops, isolated from the cybernaut in the adjoining seat, that libraries, work spaces, classrooms have become, for some of them, merely collections of individuals who are in spatial proximity but not communal propinquity, perhaps relating to someone a world away, but essentially ignorant of the person in the next seat. In a classroom of forty, my sign-up sheet may make it as far as

Preface

the sixth person, but then it sits on someone's desk, filled out but dropped like a new year's resolution into the abyss of forgotten intentions.

Undergirding these isolating or destructive changes are also alterations in the locus of authority to rule on such aberrations. Where in the past, experts were recognized in various fields and sought out to give their ruling on the truth or advisability of a suggestion or an action, today millions look elsewhere for guidance.

When the highly intelligent actor Stephen Fry, who played P.G. Wodehouse's nearly omniscient fictional character Jeeves the butler on the BBC, can sit down at his blog and find himself influencing the political thinking of a half million daily readers who have possibly confused him with Wodehouse's character, or when the artistically talented Jason Bieber can film himself in his own home and make himself as big a player on the net as the heavily investing entertainment industry could promoting the similarly talented Katy Perry, we observe an authority-making shift. The recognized pundits have been superseded by the individual entrepreneur. This is an empowering reality that makes more space on the playing fields usually dominated by well-moneyed organizations. It has elevated the individual, who can virtually run a successful enterprise on one's own—a solitary organization.

In this way, the net has distributed power for us by changing the sources of *information* and hyper-spacing niche marketing, thereby, altering the sources of *authority*. And, while this new empowering authority shift spurs competition and free enterprise, it also encourages individualism.

Today, many of us, instead of wandering next door to hail the neighbors, when we find we have a spare moment, fix ourselves before our computers, seeking fellowship

Preface

from disembodied voices in text, more real to us than folks strolling up our street, and thereby create a "community" of isolated individuals whom we may never even meet. Does this mean we are presently looking at a kind of literary "avatarism" that anticipates the complete breakdown of face-to-face, real world human interaction and, ultimately, creates the projected techno-virgins[5] who prefer machines (e.g., fembots) or game characters as mates over real humans? If so, this is clearly antithetical to what Jesus our Lord intended as Christian community. And it also ultimately undermines the idea of shared truth, making the decision of what is true Christian doctrine subject to each individual's own self (what is called in philosophy, *solipsism,* from the Latin word for solitary, *solus*, and the word for self, *ipse*, indicating oneself alone as the sole, ultimate ruler on all matters of truth). The Gospel according to me becomes the locus of authority for right doctrine; the First Church of Me becomes the determiner of right Christian practice. No wonder Jesus asked his question to resound down the ages, "When the Son of Humanity (*anthropos*) comes, will he find faith on earth?" It is a sobering thing to note that the question Jesus asks employs *ara*, an "interrogative particle expecting a negative response."[6] Jesus is not expecting a positive answer. Assessing where the future is headed, we can certainly understand why. And, we can also understand what we need to do about that prospect. As his church, we need to address it!

Addressing it is what this book is all about.

---

5. The term is the perceptive Joe Snell's in his article, "Impacts of Robotic Sex," cited in AI expert David Levy's important book, *Love and Sex with Robots: The Evolution of Human-Robot Relationships* (New York: HarperCollins, 2007), 301.

6. Newman Jr., *A Concise Greek-English Dictionary,* 24.

Preface

In the Great Commission our Lord left his disciples in Matthew 28:18–19, he commanded us who would follow him to "go, therefore, make disciples of all unbelievers" (the word here, *ethna*, means "non-Jews, Gentiles, pagans, heathen"[7]). Our task is to network everyone into the gathering of followers that Jesus began in his on-site ministry among us. But that task will not be accomplished if we are content to leave everyone to be isolated individuals, no more interacting than infants in a hospital nursery, each one of us consumed with our own needs in our own tiny bassinet.

Creative Ways to Build Christian Community is exactly what its title says it is: a very personal, practical response to the present and future prospect of isolation, a treasure trove of examples and suggestions about how to accomplish the Great Commission from community builders telling how, over the years and the ministries, they have implemented creative ways to build up churches and organizations to develop more intensive Christian fellowship and, thereby, create community. Its editors have demonstrated a long-term commitment to community building. Jeanne De Fazio is literally networked around the globe, connecting Christians together, as she divides her year between countries. Rev. John Lathrop has been a pastor for many years and is the communications coordinator between participants of the House of Priscilla and Aquila publishing line of Wipf and Stock, the publishers of this present book. Amassed in the list of contributors is a diverse group of leaders who have been building Christian community for decades. This book shares with you the innovative ideas and practices that they have used in hopes you will find it a useful tool in your own ministry. It's timely now and it will be timely in years to come.

7. Ibid.

Preface

Decades ago, I remember hearing of a survey that asked what were the two primary fears Americans had for this new millennium. The first was in the general sphere, and the answer was concern for the environment. The second was in the personal sphere, and the overwhelming response was loneliness: that each one of us would finally end up alone, our children just pictures on Facebook, disembodied voices in hurried telephone calls on Christmas and birthdays, our spouses or peers dead or isolated in senior care units as far away from us as if they'd been locked up in the dungeons of fortress keeps.

As the future continues to isolate us into solitary individuals, the Church of Jesus Christ may very well be the chief architect of face-to-face community. Because of our beliefs in a God who met us face to face and walked among us and calls us to be the body of the Christ, God's anointed one on earth, we may be the only network left standing, able completely to assure humanity that, despite the strides of artificial intelligence, the valuable work of hands, humans alone are made in the image of God and therefore never obsolete, that we are worth more than a handful of bolts.

This book will continually help remind us of that truth, as it helps us ensure a Christian communal future for humanity as well as a recognizable body of believers for our Lord when he finally comes back to gather us up to himself in God's everlasting arms of love.

William David Spencer
Ranked Adjunct Professor of Theology and the Arts,
Gordon-Conwell Theological Seminary/Boston Center for Urban Ministerial Education (CUME), Co-producer of the
House of Prisca and Aquila Series of Wipf and Stock, publishers
January 2013

Acknowledgements

A LOT OF HARD work went into making this book. It was inspired by the creative genius of Drs. William David and Aída Besançon Spencer of the House of Prisca and Aquila Series that is published by Wipf and Stock. Thank you to Dr. William David Spencer for reading the manuscript and making helpful suggestions. The text was brilliantly polished and perfected by its editors: John Lathrop and Esmé Bieberly. This book exists because of those who added their stories to mine: Teresa Flowers, Olga Soler, Jeff Marks, and Cathy Squires. Special thanks to Caleb Loring III for his support of this project.

I would like to thank my mother, Inez DeFazio for her role model of community service, my cousin Louise Maguire for her prayers, my dear friend Peggy Vanek-Titus for believing I could do it, and my precious niece Ella Louise Ryan whose prayers and love kept me going when I felt like giving up. I am indebted to my brothers, John Joseph DeFazio and Peter Francis DeFazio who helped me with the final editing. Many thanks to Shipley Walters, who inspired me to volunteer with the Davis Community Meals Program at St. Martin's Church in Davis, CA. I would like to thank Jesus most of all for his heart to serve that made this work possible.

Jeanne DeFazio

Introduction

> You are the salt of the earth. But if the salt loses its saltiness, how can it be made salty again? It is no longer good for anything, except to be thrown out and trampled underfoot. You are the light of the world. A town built on a hill cannot be hidden. Neither do people light a lamp and put it under a bowl. Instead they put it on its stand, and it gives light to everyone in the house. In the same way, let your light shine before others, that they may see your good deeds and glorify your Father in heaven. (Matthew 5:13–16 NIV)

SALT AND LIGHT IN THE CHRISTIAN COMMUNITY

WHAT DOES IT MEAN to be the "salt of the earth"? Salt preserves food from corruption and is necessary to the human diet. It had great value in ancient societies because it was less accessible than it is today. In Matthew 5:13–16, Jesus' disciples are commanded to preserve the world from general corruption and to shine forth as examples. In this way, salt and the light work together within the Christian community.

Introduction

THE CHRISTIAN COMMUNITY MUST BE EXEMPLARY

Jesus insists that Christian community "cannot be hidden" (Matt 5:14). Paul, in 1 Corinthians 12:21, tells us that people need other people. As members of the body of Christ, we experience Jesus' presence. Fellowship protects and strengthens the believer and provides him or her with an atmosphere for spiritual growth and authentic love. Christian community is a training ground for Christian leadership and is essential for the full release of spiritual gifts.

This book introduces the reader to people who are engaged in innovative ways to build Christian community. The contributors identify community as the basic structure of Christian life. Each author describes his or her personal involvement in helping develop Christian communities where brotherhood and sisterhood are lived out practically—where God's word, prayer, possessions, gifts, time, and meals have been or are still being shared. The Christian communities described in this book are

- Scripturally based.
- Historically proven to be effective for world evangelization.

BUILDING CHRISTIAN COMMUNITY THROUGH MEETINGS AND MEALS

In my chapter, "Building Christian Community Through Meetings and Meals," I highlight networking in various communities I have served, sharing my experiences of building hospitality and relational community across cultural "lines." My chapter identifies the greater evangelistic

Introduction

impact of networked communities; I explain that serving Jesus in Christian community protected me from making bad decisions and gave me great role models.

AGAPE FEASTS

In her chapter, "Agape Feasts," Teresa Flowers explains how her hospitality builds Christian community within the Pilgrim Church of Beverly, MA. The community formed by those who attend her luncheons provides a low-key, enjoyable atmosphere for relational evangelism.

THE ARTS: AN ESSENTIAL DIALOGUE FOR THE BODY OF CHRIST

In her chapter, "The Arts: An Essential Dialogue for the Body of Christ," Olga Soler addresses the subject of art as a means to build Christian community. The concern is that the arts not be seen as peripheral to the task of developing the body of Christ, but as a key means of tapping into the gifting of individuals specifically called to do various tasks of ministry: evangelism and discipleship through God's sanctioned, inspired, and directed creative expression.

A LISTENING HEART

In her chapter, "A Listening Heart," Cathy Squires demonstrates the healing aspects of community. She shows how Christians learn from one other and receive healing and support in communities. Cathy and her husband Bill lead life skill courses that are scripturally based. I have attended

Introduction

a course, and I am amazed at the insight and effectiveness of the Squires' healing courses.

A LOOK AT NEW BEGINNINGS

In his chapter, "A Look at New Beginnings," Jeff Marks tells the story of the growth of his ministry out of a home. Based on the teaching of Jesus (Matt 10:11–12), Jeff made the home a center for worship and his base for evangelization. Scriptural evangelism stemmed from Jeff's home-based community. Au pairs, college students, and Jeff's co-workers at a gas station all came to Jesus through the Bronxville Christian Fellowship that Jeff and his wife, Marjean, began in Marjean's parent's living room. Jeff chronicles the growth of a global intercessory prayer community out of this home—how yielded hearts, seeking to be continually in touch with God, can network across the world to help build local prayer communities with global reach.

PERSONAL NOTE

On a personal note, it has been one of my greatest blessings to be in Christian community with the four other contributors to this book. Jeff and Marjean Marks' New England Concerts of Prayer community has given me the opportunity to learn how to pray from anointed intercessors. Cathy and Bill Squires' life skills program has helped me to make better choices and to feel better about the choices I make. Olga Soler never ceases to amaze me with her talent to express the love and truth of Jesus through visual and performing arts. Teresa Flowers' model of Christian hospitality

Introduction

has taught me so much about feeding the body and soul of the people of Christ.

In short, a lifetime of blessings is providentially mine because of the communities represented in this book. I pray that each reader will also be blessed by these models of Christian community.

Jeanne DeFazio

1

Building Christian Community Through Meetings and Meals

Jeanne DeFazio

OVER THE COURSE OF the last four decades I have been privileged to be involved in several Christian communities. The experiences that I have had, both building and participating in these groups, have become a multicolored tapestry woven together by the power of the Holy Spirit. These communities have truly touched my heart and soul with the love of Jesus. The ministries I served brought me into a wonderful company of highly creative, intelligent, and spiritually strong Christian men and woman. As I share the memories of these times when Jesus touched my life in Hollywood, New York City, Washington, DC, and London, England, I pray that you too will experience some of the joy I received while serving Jesus.

WORLD ALLIANCE FOR PEACE BIBLE STUDIES IN HOLLYWOOD

From 1983 to 1995, I worked as an administrative assistant for Mr. M. P. Grace II. One of my duties was to organize a Bible study that was attended by members of the entertainment industry. Mr. Grace was a prominent and devout Roman Catholic. His close friend, actress Christine White, encouraged him to become a born-again Christian, which he did. This spiritual awakening brought him great joy as he experienced the forgiveness of sins and was filled with the love and power of Jesus. Mr. Grace's born-again experience motivated him to sponsor meetings so that others could receive new lives in Jesus. His devoted friend, the veteran actress, Joan Caufield, noticed the spiritual growth in him and encouraged his outreaches. The Bible studies took place in Mr. Grace's homes in Playa del Rey and Mandeville Canyon. Over the years, the venue had to be changed to banquet rooms in local Hollywood hotels in order to accommodate the number of attendees.

These meetings were sponsored by World Alliance for Peace. Charlene Eber, secretary and director of advertising for WAPF, explains,

> I had the privilege to volunteer as secretary and director of advertising for 14 years with World Alliance for Peace. The inspiration for it was a phenomenal experience. A voice in the night woke me with a message, part of which was, "We are the children. We are the world. This world does not belong to us. It belongs to our children and our children's children. We are merely caretakers of the future. We need to start making a difference now." I shared this with Michael Grace the next day, and his response was that we have to do something with it. Together, we came up with the name, World Alliance for Peace. He brought the idea to Archbishop Metropolitan John Stanley, founder of the Orthodox Church of the East. Our vision was that the whole world is our community, as we are all God's children and we are all responsible for each other. We met with Major General Uban in India and helped initiate peace talks between India and Pakistan and were able to get medical equipment donated

to the Okanarth Health Center and much-needed medicine and assistance to Mother Teresa. Our primary focus was on helping grassroots types of organizations that desperately needed help, including Christian missionary groups such as Breath of the Spirit and later, Christ in You, the Hope of Glory.[1]

Joanne Petronella and her daughter, Michelle Corral, faithful and loving Christian friends to Mr. Grace, are both powerful ministers of Jesus' redemptive love. They attended Mr. Grace's meetings and opened the door for many members of their own ministries, Christ in You, the Hope of Glory and Breath of Spirit respectively, to bond spiritually with the regular attendees of Mr. Grace's monthly Bible studies.

A wonderful and culturally diverse Christian community developed as a result of these meetings. Michael Roemer, a devout Catholic, attended one of Mr. Grace's Hollywood meetings. The community included actress Jane Ross, and Mr. Grace's confidant, actress Midori Arimoto. His colleague Barbara Evans introduced him to Prophetess Ada Schwartz. Ada ministered at several of Mr. Grace's meetings. The late Mary Dorr and Gordon Gordon, founders of Excellence in Media, honored Mr. Grace with an Angel Award; they were strong supporters of his ministry to the Hollywood community.

Pastor Robert Reith, of Media Fellowship International, faithfully took time from his own ministerial responsibilities to encourage those who attended the meetings with insights from Scripture. Many talented vocalists led the

1. Charlene Eber, July 2012. Interview by telephone and email with author. Charlene Eber confirmed that she was in communication with Ken Kragen's office and that Mr. Kragen's office expressed interest in her peace project prior to Michael Jackson and Lionel Ritchie's hit song, "We Are the World."

worship. Among them were actress, author, and songstress, Maria St. John (who often hosted these events) and actress and songstress, Miss Mayrita Varna. Those who were weary in spirit found solace in Pastor Reith's teaching and the encouragement of the worship. One person who was especially faithful to the monthly meeting was Wally Bruder. Wally shared Jesus' love by hugging everyone who attended and by faithfully praying for their concerns. In his own words, "It was a privilege and joy being part of this group where together we were encouraged and richly blessed in pursuing the priceless treasure of being drawn deep into the heart of Jesus first for our own edification, and out of the overflow we freely shared Jesus' transforming love, joy, peace, and presence with everyone else."[2]

Beulah Bee Beyer Wenger, editor of the *Hollywood Times,* and her daughter Gemma, producer of the international television series, *Hollywood* and *Beauty for Ashes,* brought members of the entertainment industry to the event. Beulah Bee Beyer Wenger remembers Mr. Grace: "As in biblical times, many were named according to their character; Michael Grace was also appropriately named because he was constantly helping people to become Christians and to lead them to God's amazing grace."[3]

Gemma Wenger recalls Mr. Grace's influence upon her a young child:

> As a young child, I remember Mr. Grace gathering people together in churches, restaurants, and homes to hear and grow in the word of God. He was a pioneer in bringing the gifts of the Spirit to people who were hungry for a deeper walk with the Lord. The seeds that were planted in my heart through Mr. Grace's outreach have

2. Wally Bruder, interview by email with author, August 2012.
3. Beulah Bee Beyer, interview by email with author, July 2012.

> resulted in me starting my own evangelical and prophetic international ministry. Mr. Grace was a friend, a leader, and a spiritual guide to a body of people called by God. He truly was raised up for a specific time and a purpose to break the bonds of religious tradition and usher in a new era of God's anointing.[4]

All who attended the meetings were invited to have a light supper hosted by World Alliance for Peace, which I was responsible to organize and cater. These were very informal and nontraditional events. No one was judged by appearance or lifestyle; all were greeted with love and acceptance and were made to feel welcome in Jesus. Relationships formed, and many of those who attended accepted Jesus as Lord and Savior and subsequently sought fellowship in local churches. Mr. Grace's Hollywood outreach continued until his passing in May 1995.

During these years of service, I developed close relationships with many people who were from totally different backgrounds than I was. I had been brought up in a small university town and led a fairly sheltered childhood. Many of those who came to these events suffered from addictions and poor relationship choices. I learned to be open-minded and open-hearted and grew to love so many of these dear and wonderful Christians. This ministry impacted me deeply. I still have close friends from this community, and I draw on their spiritual strength as prayer warriors. The prayer materials that I receive from Pastor Mel Novak, who is an actor and the founder of Heavenly Manna Inc.—especially his "Arsenal of Protection and Deliverance"—are part of my daily intercession. Mel's newsletters and reports of numerous conversions among the imprisoned and those on skid row have been a great encouragement to me.

4. Gemma Wenger, interview by email with author, July 2012.

Creative Ways to Build Christian Community

Beulah Bee Beyer Wenger has been a great support to me as an author. She placed advertisements in the *Hollywood Times* for a book I coauthored with Teresa Flowers, entitled *How to Have an Attitude of Gratitude on the Night Shift*. Bee is a member of the Southern California Motion Picture Council, which has twice honored me with Lifetime Charitable Achievement Awards. Mary Dorr, of Excellence in Media, honored me with an Angel Award for Lifetime Charitable Achievement. Joanne Petronella twice invited me to travel to India with her ministry, Christ in You, the Hope of Glory to minister with Mother Teresa and the Sisters of Charity. Bishop John Stanley invited me to travel to Israel on a missionary tour. These were life-changing experiences. Throughout the years, Bob Reith of Media Fellowship International has remembered me in his prayer-chain emails and met with me for counseling, in New York City, Washington, DC, and London, England. In retrospect I can say that my life has been changed for the better because of this company of Christians whose devotion to Jesus and commitment to fulfilling the Great Commission is outstanding. Charlene Eber's words capture the excitement of this communal ministry:

> We could all ask God to reveal what our soul intention is. He will answer. Every community needs help. It may be in your own backyard, or in the missionary field, or by starting a Bible study in your area. You can make a difference, and no effort is too small. In our journey, every step we take forward, God opens another door, and we are blessed enough to be able to walk through and share an incredible journey of faith. There are no words to sum up how amazing an opportunity it is to walk in faith and inspire others around you. There is no greater joy than serving God and helping humanity. I promise you, if you

take a step in this direction, you are in for the greatest time of your life. It certainly has been mine. God bless you all the days of your life.[5]

WORLD ALLIANCE FOR PEACE NEW YORK CITY BIBLE STUDIES

By 1986, I was working as Mr. Grace's executive assistant in both New York City and Los Angeles. I had a hectic schedule with great responsibilities administering to Mr. Grace's legal, banking, social, and charitable activities. I was reluctant to take on any more responsibility, but Mr. Grace directed me to organize his World Alliance for Peace New York City Bible study. Mr. Grace's longtime friend, realtor Ann Pett, introduced him to New York City inventor, consultant, and entrepreneur, Dr. Robert Fondillier. Dr. Fondiller graciously hosted a monthly prayer meeting in his apartment on West 58th Street, NYC, for Mr. Grace. After these meetings, the attendees were invited to a supper hosted by Mr. Grace and World Alliance for Peace at a local restaurant. Bishop Singh, a colleague of Ann Pett, led these monthly meetings at Dr. Fondillier's home. He also conducted a weekly outreach sponsored by World Alliance for Peace. The outreach was held at a McDonald's Restaurant in New York's Broadway theater district for anyone who needed a meal, prayer, or spiritual encouragement. Due to the growth of these ministries, the venue was changed to the third floor of the McDonald's Restaurant on 58th Street and Third Avenue. I purchased meal tickets from McDonald's which were distributed free to all who attended the monthly meeting. Pastor Robert Reith of Media Fellowship International encouraged this group with Scripture.

5. Charlene Eber, interview by email with author, July 2012.

Encouragement, as Hollywood Circus of the Stars stuntman Bob Yerkes explains, is one of Pastor Bob's great gifts: "Pastor Bob Reith is down to earth and kind. He listens and encourages us, sharing Scripture praying with and for us. Under his pastoral anointing, we bond and feel great joy in Christian community devoted to bringing others to Jesus."[6]

The culturally diverse attendees worshipped God in song and testified of his grace. An unusual community developed; it included friends of Mr. Grace from society and the business world as well as homeless people from the West 51st Street Baptist Mission. Each meeting was filmed by New York City filmmaker, Oscar Marquez. Copies of these films were distributed to those who were unable to attend the meetings.

This event made a huge difference in my life. As I mentioned earlier, when Mr. Grace asked me to organize this event, I already had a lot of additional responsibilities; I administered all of Mr. Grace's Los Angeles business and social activities as well as his monthly trips between New York City and Los Angeles. I also organized his international trips to India and Israel. In view of these responsibilities, I did not feel that I could organize another event. However, as time went on I began to look forward to the McDonald's restaurant Bible study each month. This Christian community was novel in that it broke down social barriers and brought people from various walks of life together to worship Jesus. At these meetings, friendships developed between those who had previously felt uncomfortable within the traditional churches. The homeless no longer felt isolated. The hearts of those who attended the meetings felt the presence and love of God that was developing in the Christian community. Mr. Grace's dear friend,

---

6. Bob Yerkes, interview by telephone with author, July 2012.

actress, author, and political activist, April Shenandoah, puts it perfectly:

> Show business was my God until I met God! During those years in Hollywood, and New York, I attended several Media Fellowship International meetings conducted by Michael Grace. Being a new Christian, I soaked up more godly wisdom at those gatherings than I was aware of at the time. Michael Grace was born with just the right name. He offered "GRACE" to "ALL." His ministry to the homeless was heartfelt, as I had the pleasure of experiencing firsthand in Manhattan—upstairs at a McDonald's restaurant. Thank God for the vision that Michael Grace had for others.[7]

MEDIA FELLOWSHIP INTERNATIONAL'S HIGH-PROFILE CHRISTIAN TESTIMONIAL LUNCHEONS SPONSORED BY WORLD ALLIANCE FOR PEACE

In the early 1990s, Pastor Robert Reith's Media Fellowship International hosted The New York City high-profile Christian Testimonial Luncheons which were sponsored by World Alliance for Peace. These events were held quarterly at prominent New York locations, including Sardi's Restaurant, Mickey Mantle's Restaurant, the Armory, and the Soldiers, Sailors, and Airmen's Club. Guests heard powerful Christian testimonies from baseball legend Bobby Richardson; Chaplain Susan Stafford, PhD, best known as the original Wheel of Fortune hostess who was a young pioneer for women in game shows and is today a humanitarian and

---

7. April Shenandoah, interview by email with author, May 2012.

author;[8] J.J. Ebaugh of CNN; Governor of Missouri, John Ashcroft (who later became the U.S. Attorney General); and international songstress Martha Reyes. Among those in attendance were Ben Bradlee of the *Washington Post;* Tony Duke, founder of Boys and Girls Harbor; Cy Block of the Israel Children's Center; Ted Baehr, founder of *MovieGuide*; Harriet Nesbitt, artist and founder of Mothers for More Halfway Houses; Miss Joanne La Placa, celebrity photographer, author, songwriter, and social activist; Lady Allison Assante; columnist Marilyn Vos Savant; Monsignor Avery Dulles (who later became Cardinal Dulles); Mr. Grace's cousin, Morgan Grace; baseball legend, Mickey Mantle; and Mr. Grace's dear friend, actress Tina Louise. Staff members of *Guideposts* magazine attended the event regularly. Mr. Grace's social stature drew distinguished members of New York society and the business world to these events, and the Holy Spirit touched the hearts of those who attended with powerful testimonies of Christian faith. The events were filmed, and the tapes were distributed to those who were not able to attend.

In preparation for these luncheons, I had to print and send out invitations, arrange seating, select appropriate venues, organize menus, and hire a filmmaker to film each event. It was an awesome responsibility, and I learned much from it. I saw highly sophisticated non-Christians touched by the presence of the Holy Spirit and the love of Jesus through witness and prayer. Community developed to such a degree that those who were normally uncomfortable with public prayer or worship outside of the traditional church gained strength and solace from it. The Holy Spirit

8. Susan Stafford, interview by email with author, July 2012. Susan Stafford went on to work with cancer, leprosy, and AIDS patients. Her favorite saying is "Religion is for the birds, and Jesus is for the people."

Building Christian Community Through Meetings and Meals

used songs to soften hearts for Jesus' message. Many people who were insulated by prominence and good fortune were moved to make Jesus real in their lives. I realized then that Jesus could open any heart. This gave me confidence to pray for those I would not have considered asking God to save. June George, a devout Roman Catholic, attended an MFI Washington, DC, event and was delighted with the spiritual caliber of MFI's members, and Pastor Bob Reith's devotion to bring souls to Jesus touched her heart.[9] Lord John Taylor, Lord of Warwick summed up the international influence of MFI: "I have participated in Media Fellowship International events for the last 12 years. During that space of time, I have become close to many Christians who have impacted my spiritual life deeply. Pastor Bob Reith has been highly creative and effective in building Christian community worldwide."[10]

Pastor Bob Reith also commented on the impact of the MFI NYC events:

> Michael Grace could truly be called a "character"—he was one of a kind. He had a burning passion to bring the gospel of Jesus Christ to everyone, especially to those who were either "up and out" or "down and out." He had a different idea of how that should be done. Michael arranged for Christian meetings to be held at a wide variety of locations, including the best restaurants, fine homes, and miscellaneous public places. I remember speaking at Sardi's Restaurant one day and in the main room at McDonald's in New York City on another.

---

9. June George, interview in person with author, February 2010.

10. Lord John Taylor, Lord of Warwick, House of Lords, Parliament, London, England, interview by email with author, July 2012.

Creative Ways to Build Christian Community

> Michael wasn't a preacher, but he was instrumental in bringing hundreds of souls to Christ because he arranged, or rather Jeanne DeFazio arranged, meetings that brought together people who were hungry for the Lord, and often hungry for a good meal, with successful people in sports, entertainment, business, or politics who had a strong Christian testimony. This outreach continued for many years, mainly in Los Angeles and New York. He had a vision and a mission to see people saved.
>
> Michael called on Media Fellowship International and Pastor Bob Rieth to help with this missionary effort. MFI is a ministry that reaches out to the secular media and entertainment community with the goal of introducing individuals to Jesus, nurturing them as they learn God's Word and encouraging them as they walk with God in their professional and personal lives. It was a privilege and a blessing to be able to partner with him to preach and to teach the saving Word of the Lord to the people that Michael invited in from the highways and byways to come and sit at the table and be fed the Word.[11]

Subsequently, in 2004 and 2010, I have had the opportunity to volunteer with the Holy Trinity, Brompton's Alpha Program[12] in London England. I mention this program and its founder Vicar Nicky Gumbel as the program is similar to MP Grace II's outreach format. Both have succeeded in bringing the upscale and unchurched into

---

11. Reverend Robert Reith, interview by email with author, July 2012.

12. Web site: www.htb.org.uk, viewed September 12, 2012.

Christian community with a supper program that outlines basic Christianity.

HEAVENLY MANNA INC.

Mel Novak's ministry, Heavenly Manna Inc., has greatly impacted my life. Mel is a dedicated soldier of Christ, an ordained minister called by God to share the Good News of salvation in Jesus Christ with the homeless on skid row and in the prisons. He reaches out to those that many people do not want to have anything to do with. His ministry is unique in that it builds Christian community among the helpless and hopeless: those who have nothing and no one. For the past thirty years, Mel has faithfully ministered at Los Angeles rescue missions, and for the past twenty-seven years, he has also ministered in penitentiaries nationwide. Through Mel's ministry, thousands have accepted God's precious gift of salvation through grace, by receiving Jesus Christ as their Lord and Savior or rededicating their lives to Jesus. Mel's deliverance and protection prayers build Christian community within the walls of penal institutions and among the homeless.

Building Christian Community Through Intercessory Prayer

Sixteen years ago, Mel gave me a copy of his Arsenal of Prayers.[13] These prayers are the backbone of his ministry. Saying these prayers daily for the past sixteen years has changed my life. I have emailed these prayers to those in need and prayed for people in groups using the Arsenal

---

13. Web site: melnovak.com/arsenal.htm, viewed September 11, 2012.

Prayers. I believe that these scripturally based prayers are effective in providing protection and deliverance and also in building Christian community. Several thousands of copies of Arsenal Prayers have been distributed to date. Arsenal Prayers have helped build Christian community in a unique way. Thousands of intercessors repeat these prayers daily. Members of national prayer chains use this miraculous arsenal of prayers to begin their intercession for the lost. Many people bound by torment and despair within the penitentiary walls and in homeless camps in the inner city say these arsenal prayers and are released from isolation and come into community with Jesus and others. Mel's Arsenal Prayers have an anointing that sets captives free and brings the lost to Jesus and into Christian community. "Mel has been a member of the Academy of Motion Picture Arts for 17 years."[14] Thousands have found Christ through his preaching and teaching.[15] Mel says that he is not the one doing the work: "I give God the honor, worship, and glory... So I count it an honor and privilege to be able to share my faith and lead lost souls to Christ. The Lord truly blesses me as I serve Him in whatever way He leads."[16]

CHRIST IN YOU, THE HOPE OF GLORY

In 1987 and 1989, I had the privilege of traveling to India, Singapore, and Bangkok, Thailand, in ministry with Dr. Joanne Petronella. This experience rocked my life. Dr. Petronella is the founder of Christ in You, the Hope of Glory, a ministry based in Brea, CA. Her international ministry has brought the lost to Jesus in India, Singapore,

14. Web site: http://melnovak.com/index2.html, viewed February 12, 2013.
15. Ibid.
16. Ibid.

Building Christian Community Through Meetings and Meals

Jordan, Israel, Africa, and Russia. For the past thirty years she has led a reenactment of Jesus' final steps to his crucifixion on Good Friday on the Via Dolorosa, in the Old City of Jerusalem in Israel. In 2012, Jaron Gilinski filmed her Good Friday processional, and the film has appeared on Time.com internationally.[17] Visit the link in the footnote and see for yourself the distinct and unforgettable way in which her ministry touches hearts with the passion of Jesus. Onlooker's hearts are moved by Jesus' great sacrifice. Dr. Petronella's Good Friday Pilgrimage is a very creative way to build Christian community.

The Good Friday Pilgrimage

As was mentioned above, Christ in You, the Hope of Glory ministry has been doing the Good Friday pilgrimage for thirty years. Each Good Friday, the ministry team walks on the ancients stones of the Way of Sorrows to acknowledge Jesus' death and resurrection as the key to salvation. They sing hymns and carry large wooden crosses, marching in solemn processions retracing Jesus' final steps to his crucifixion. Members of Dr. Petronella's ministry team from Southern California travel the Via Dolorosa, in costume, and re-enact Jesus' final walk. Each Good Friday, Dr. Petronella is certain that God hears her prayers spoken along the Way of Sorrows for the peoples of the world. She feels a great connection with God, as she prays for the nations to come to Jesus. Her prayers along the Way of Suffering build Christian community in the spiritual realm. This is a pilgrimage of faith. Those who respond to the agony of Jesus as represented by this pilgrimage recognize Jesus' sacrifice and are reminded that his stripes and precious blood saved

17. "Californians Bring Passion," TIME.com.

humankind from the consequences of sin. All who receive Jesus as their Lord and Savior have access to the Heavenly Father and the power of the Holy Spirit. This reenactment of the Passion of Jesus calls attention to these spiritual realities. Cameras flash as onlookers view Jesus and are reminded of his love.

The Good Friday reenactment builds community among the onlookers in a powerful way. The tone is solemn, and the presence of Jesus is evident and often accompanied by the aroma of the Rose of Sharon from the Garden of Gethsemane. This is a mystical reminder of Jesus' precious blood poured out to redeem humankind. The response to the Good Friday pilgrimage is solemn. Strangers' awareness of Jesus' presence draws them together. They respond to one another with the awareness that Jesus died for them. Emotions are evident as Jesus touches each heart with the message of his redemptive love. Dr. Petronella's ministry travels eagerly to Jerusalem each year to train the team to re-enact Jesus' final steps. The team prays in costume for the hearts that will be touched by him and receive him along those ancient stone steps. Team members share hotel rooms and return from the pilgrimage with the experience of touching hearts for Jesus. The experience binds team members together with a certainty that they are fulfilling the great commission to bring the lost to Jesus in a creative and compelling way.

In retrospect, I realized how blessed I was to network with all of these Christian ministries due to my introductory experience organizing Mr. Grace's community ministry meal programs.

Building Christian Community Through Meetings and Meals

U.S. SENATE CHAPLAIN LLOYD OGILVIE'S FRIDAY AFTERNOON LUNCHEON AND BIBLE STUDY FOR THE STAFF AT THE UNITED STATES SENATE

From 1999 to 2001, while I was a staff assistant at the Environment and Public Works Committee of the U.S. Senate, I attended United States Senate Chaplain Lloyd Ogilvie's Friday afternoon staff meetings. The community that developed among the regular attendees of this gathering became a great source of spiritual support. Chaplain Ogilvie's teaching, which was often preceded by worship led by Christian vocalist Wintley Phipps, was inspirational. The Environment and Public Works staff faced many challenges. Each Friday, I listened closely to the chaplain's teaching for spiritual direction. It was always simple, straightforward, and powerful. Many times, he spoke on the book of John, exhorting all who attended to heed the apostle's words and to love one another. Upon returning to my office after the meetings, I found myself praising Jesus because I was able to feel compassion toward other staff members in a new and deeper way. This compassion grew from the love of God that Chaplain Ogilvie spoke about at each meeting.

Chaplain Ogilvie built Christian community in the workplace. Jesus walked through those halls, and many times Ogilvie carried the staff in attendance through great political turbulence. He stood in the gap for Senate staff members on Friday afternoons. In his own words,

> It is not surprising that I am deeply committed to Bible studies and small fellowship groups meeting in the secular world. I became a Christian as a freshman in college. An informal Bible study and discussion group met down the hall from my dormitory room. After listening in

Creative Ways to Build Christian Community

on the communication of a dynamic quality of Christianity, I made my commitment to Christ. The group nurtured me in my first steps of following the Savior. Since then, I have never been without my own group of covenant brothers and sisters who meet to share the adventure and accountability of discipleship.

That's the reason that, during fifty-five years of ministry, I have felt called to equip and encourage people to live out their faith in government, business, education, entertainment, various professions, and in their families. In addition to caring for them personally, I have been committed to developing Bible studies and small groups to provide mutual support and strength for them to be faithful and effective disciples.

Most people work about 160,000 hours during their lifetime. Those who take few vacations and work after hours will work about 200,000 hours. A housewife will work more than 290,000! Work can be a false god and the object of worship. The challenge for most Christians is to bring meaning to their work rather than making their work the primary meaning of their lives. To do that, they need other believers with whom they can meet consistently to deepen their faith through study of the Scriptures, sharing of hopes and needs, and prayer for each other. There should be no solo flights for those who are committed to Christ, who need fresh grace for daily living under the plumb line of His righteousness, who need courage to seek His guidance for crucial decisions, and who long to communicate their faith, hope, and love to others who also struggle in the strain and stress of secular life.

Building Christian Community Through Meetings and Meals

In each of the churches I have served as pastor, I have witnessed firsthand the power of Christians meeting together in the business community, in colleges and universities, in the movie industry, and in homes and neighborhoods. The basic purpose of these dynamic fellowship groups has been to enable people to press on with wisdom, vision, courage, and supernatural power.

One of the most challenging areas to serve is in government, particularly in Washington, DC. I have come to believe that being an elected member of the Congress or to serve on his or her staff is a very high calling. When I was elected to serve as the 61st United States Senate Chaplain, I felt that my primary purpose was to encourage our leaders and their staffs to grow in their relationship with the Lord, the Sovereign of our Nation, and to seek His will in the monumental responsibilities and soul-sized decisions entrusted to them. In addition to opening the Senate each day in prayer, my privilege was to be an intercessor for the Senators and their families, a trusted prayer partner, and a faithful spiritual counselor.

During my ten years as chaplain (1995–2003), I had five major Bible studies each week: the Senators met on Thursday, the Senators' spouses on Tuesday, the Chiefs of Staff on Wednesday, and two staff groups, one on Tuesday and the other on Friday. The great Scriptures of the Old and New Testament were shared in an effort to empower the Senators and their staffs both personally and professionally. In addition, small groups were formed in offices for in-depth reflection and prayer. These groups were called the H.O.S.I.—the Holy Order of Senate Intercessors. Leaders of these groups were trained, and

> materials for discussion were provided. These spiritually empowered, morally rooted, ethically focused men and women meet together for inspired introspection and vision, and then press on with integrity, imagination, and the impelling inspiration of the Holy Spirit in the crucial realms of responsibility where they have been divinely deployed to serve.
>
> I saw my role as chaplain to be non-political, non-partisan and non-sectarian. With our heritage as Americans, there never can be a separation of God and state! I was deeply honored to follow Dr. Richard Halverson in the chaplaincy and to be succeeded by Dr. Barry Black, both truly great spiritual enablers of those who are called to serve in government.[18]

YVONNE O'NEAL

Yvonne O'Neal is the founder of My Child Ministry, a non-profit organization. She has developed cross-cultural Christian community in a very creative way. Over the past thirty years she has worked for and volunteered with various programs primarily in Southeast Washington, DC, and abroad. It has been my privilege to experience unique multicultural Christian community as I participated in the various programs she has directed.

Frederick Douglass Center

When I first met Yvonne in 1997, she brought me to the Frederick Douglass Child Development Center in

---

18. Dr. Lloyd Ogilvie, interview by email with author, July 2012.

Building Christian Community Through Meetings and Meals

Southeast Washington, DC. As its former director, she implemented child care that was effective in the development of inner-city children. The Frederick Douglass Center provides preschool and after-school child care for children of women who are often single, working African Americans. It is not affiliated with a church but receives support from local Southeast churches. I mention the center in this chapter because the churches that support the child care program form a community of Christians whose outreach in the secular community is essential. In addition to applying for federal, state, and civic grants to provide funding for Frederick Douglass Day Care, Yvonne also worked with local Christian communities that helped the program with materials and funding. The Christian Community that developed as a result of her networking with inner-city churches to support the Frederick Douglass Center brought food, clothing, and medical services and essential prayer support to that center.

Fishing School

The Fishing School is located on Meade Street in Northeast Washington, DC. In the 1990s, I often went there. Yvonne worked for Mr. Tom Lewis, who founded the school. This private school teaches skills and provides mentoring for inner-city youth. Meeting Tom Lewis made a difference in my life. It was clear that he stood up for and made a difference in the lives of many inner-city children who could have gone the wrong way without his support and example. A former DC police officer and a strong Christian, Mr. Lewis helps break the cycle of poverty by providing computer skills and guidance for Southeast DC youth.

Mr. Lewis has distinguished himself in Christian service. The school applies Christian principles to the education of inner-city youth who often live at a poverty level. As an instructor and a liaison to the Fishing School, Yvonne built Christian community by working with local churches and Christian organizations that helped supply funds and food for the school. While working for Mr. Lewis, she learned to preach the gospel and to use words to do so only when necessary.[19]

Little White House of Southeast, DC

Located on Pennsylvania Avenue, in Southeast Washington, DC, this ministry is affectionately known in the neighborhood as the Little White House due to its distinctive architecture and its location four miles east of the "real" White House. Rather than a political seat of power, however, the Little White House is a resource center serving the needs of the community's youth with mentoring, skill training, and cultural programs for artistic and performing arts instruction. It is referred to as a "house on a hill for all people" as it is a gathering place for all those working with the poor and disenfranchised of the community. In the 1990s Yvonne O'Neal served as a liaison with the Little White House, building Christian community with local churches and Christian non-profits that developed arts programs for inner-city adults and children. This Christian community brought lifestyle changes, jobs, fellowship and friendship, and most of all Jesus' love to rich and poor, black and white, young and old.[20]

---

19. Web site: http://www.fishingschool.org/, viewed September 10, 2012.

20. Web site: http://sewhitehouse.org/about.asp, viewed September 10, 2012.

Building Christian Community Through Meetings and Meals

All-Night Praise-a-Thons at the Lincoln Memorial

The Lincoln Memorial is located on Lincoln Memorial Circle SW in Washington, DC. It is an architectural anchor for the west end of the Washington Mall on the grassy area between the Capitol Building and the Potomac River. At this historic and famous site at the onset of the millennium, Yvonne O'Neal produced two all-night Praise-a Thons, providing worship music sung by local inner-city Washington, DC, youth choirs. These events developed Christian community among the DC youth who participated in ringing in the millennium by performing Christian worship music.

My Child Ministry National Prayer Line

Since 2008, Yvonne O'Neal has directed a national prayer conference call line with as many as nine participants per night. Participants call, log in with a pin number, and then join the conference call each night at midnight Eastern Standard Time. Members of the prayer line are located on the East and West coasts of the United States. These people represent diverse cultural backgrounds. Each night the prayer team begins to pray by reciting the Lord's Prayer. Members of the prayer team (including Yvonne O'Neal, Jackie Davidson, Linda Lockhart, Julia Davis, Jean Barboza, Andrea Fong, Louise Maguire, and Jeanne DeFazio) worship the Lord in song, share Scriptures, testify, give praise reports, and offer petitions on behalf of those in need of prayer. Members of the prayer line have experienced miraculous answers to prayer. A Christian community has developed on this prayer line among those who intercede regularly.

Creative Ways to Build Christian Community

The Bible as an Elective Program

Since 2010, Yvonne O'Neal has advocated the teaching of the Bible as an elective in the DC school curriculum. This program has been a highly creative way to build Christian community nationally. Yvonne has prayed and worked with many Christians in various states who have been able to succeed in bringing the study of the Bible as an elective into their local public school curriculums.

Summary of Yvonne O'Neal's Ministries

God in his infinite wisdom develops cross-cultural Christian community to edify the church. God has used Yvonne's personal history, social skills, and spiritual gifts to break down the walls of prejudice and build cross-cultural Christian community. As an African-American child, at the height of the civil rights movement in Mississippi, Yvonne was integrated into all-white schools. This experience taught her to relate to the individual independent of race, color, or creed. In Southeast Washington, DC, as a young adult on staff at the Frederick Douglass Center and the Fishing School, her ethnic background gave her the education and social skills necessary to teach the predominately African-American inner-city students how to develop in order to succeed in a multicultural society.

In the late 1990s, Yvonne was a liaison for a Southeast DC Arts program developed through the Little White House in the Southeast, Washington, DC. Networking with many Christian artists and philanthropists from diverse cultural backgrounds, the Little White House in the Southeast DC neighborhood set high standards that helped break cultural barriers and promote multicultural community. The added component of the love of Jesus embodied in the

Building Christian Community Through Meetings and Meals

soul, spirit, and visual expression of the Christian artists who participated in that program provided a spiritual depth that benefited the adults and children of the Southeast DC neighborhood. This project modeled God's development of cross-cultural Christian community at its best. In 2004, Yvonne ministered in England to the predominately white and upper-class members of Holy Trinity Brompton at their Alpha Marriage and Prison Ministry conferences. She, along with other Christians from diverse nationalities and cultural backgrounds, broke ground for the development of a cross-cultural Christian community interceding at St. Paul's Church during J. John's "Just 10" revival. At the "Soul in the City" tent revival at Clapham Common that same summer, Yvonne and I served supper with Christians from every nationality and cultural background to thousands of souls that the Holy Spirit directed into that tent to hear Mike Pilavachi call them home to Jesus. These are some examples of the ways in which God continues to use Yvonne's personal history, social skills, and spiritual gifts to break down the walls of prejudice and build cross-cultural Christian community.

In 2005, I was honored to attend a Southern California Motion Picture Arts Council Award luncheon with Yvonne. At that event she received the Southern California Motion Picture Arts Council Life Time Charitable Achievement Award. As I sat at the table and listened to her speak, I became aware that God brought this saint of the church into my life from her Mississippi background; she has enriched my life by helping me understand how to override cultural barriers with the grace of God in order to help fulfill the great mission of the church: the Great Commission.

CONCLUSION: RECOMMENDATIONS FOR BUILDING CHRISTIAN COMMUNITIES

God, who is the source of all creativity, builds Christian community through the unique gifting of his people. In this chapter, I have mentioned a number of creative ways in which Christian communities were built through meetings. Two of the ministries I helped organize, Mr. Grace's Hollywood and New York City outreaches, and a number I participated in—Nicky Gumbel's Alpha Program, Mel Novak's Heavenly Manna Inc., Dr. Joanne Petronella's Christ in You, the Hope of Glory Ministry, Chaplain Lloyd Ogilvie's Friday afternoon staff meetings at the U.S. Senate, and a number of ministries with Yvonne O'Neal.

It would be easy for these prominent and strong Christian men and women who have been kind enough to comment in this chapter to tell you that I was not a strong Christian when I began organizing or participating in these Christian communities. Exposure to these ministries put me in fellowship with strong Christian believers. These associations helped to develop my Christian character and kept me out of a lot of trouble. These communities were God's precious gifts to me. My life has been transformed by Christian service and membership in Christian community. I hope and pray that you too have already, or will, experience the joy and love of Jesus, and grow in the knowledge of his grace through similar involvement in active Christian community.

2

Agape Feasts

Teresa Two Feathers Flowers

"The Kitchen Prayer"
I thank You, Father, for the dirty pots and pans in the sink.
You have allowed me to feed someone.
I thank You, Father, for the fellowship.
You have allowed me to befriend someone.
I thank You, Father, for the warmth of Your Love.
You have allowed me to share with someone.
I thank You, Lord, for the smells in the kitchen that draw people in.
You have allowed me to share Your Love.[1]

Teresa Flowers

INTRODUCTION

I ARRIVED IN BEVERLY, Massachusetts ten years ago. From 2002 to 2008, I served as a Night Caretaker for troubled boys at Anchorage House in Beverly and a Day Caretaker for at-risk and abused children at Star House in Beverly. I cooked at Anchorage House and Star House for the children under my care. From 2011 to the present, I have served as a

1. Flowers and DeFazio, *Attitude of Gratitude*, 2011.

monitor for disabled children for First Call Transportation Service.

For the past ten years, I have attended Pilgrim Church in Beverly, serving the community as a deacon, elder and, as of 2008, as the Director of the Pilgrim Church Community Meals Program. Under my direction, Pilgrim Church sponsors a free hot lunch from September 1st through June 1st. In addition to lunch, guests receive pastries and breads donated by Panera Bread and delivered to Pilgrim Church by Deacon Douglas MacDougal. Elder Sophia Obeke insists that her grandchildren are eager to attend Pilgrim Church because they love the bagels and desserts from Panera.

SCRIPTURAL FOCUS OF THE PILGRIM CHURCH COMMUNITY MEALS PROGRAM

> They devoted themselves to the apostles' teaching and to fellowship, to the breaking of bread and to prayer. (Acts 2:42 NIV)

The word of God encourages Christians to share meals. In the line of apostolic example of Acts 2:42, the Pilgrim Church community meals program enabled everyone to come to the table to fellowship, break bread, and pray. It is in this spirit of the early church that I provide a hospitality program to the community in Beverly. Olga Soler observes that "eating together and doing things together is the most church-like thing we do. The early church did more of that than anything else. They ministered to each other during meals. Communion or breaking bread together was not just a sip of grape juice and a morsel of bread; it was a meal."[2]

---

2. Olga Soler, interview with author by email, June 2012.

Agape Feasts

I make it a point to welcome everyone to lunch for prayer, fellowship, and fun as an enactment of Jesus' command that Christians "love one another" (John 13:34 NIV). This is a true ministry of joy and welcome inviting those of all ages, cultures, and talents fulfilling Jesus' prayer in John 17:23: "that [we] may be brought to complete unity."

In her August 10, 2011, front-page article in the *Beverly Citizen*, Deborah Gardner Walker noted that my lunches were open to all: "Flowers continues to offer love, hope, and food to the disenfranchised in Beverly. She prepares a free lunch after Sunday worship at Pilgrim Church on Cabot Street, feeding church members and anyone else who want to come."[3]

HOW DOES THE PILGRIM CHURCH COMMUNITY MEALS PROGRAM OPERATE?

The Pilgrim Church Community Meals Program is sponsored by private donations and the Pilgrim Church Deacon's Fund. Prior to the weekly meal, I organize the menu, purchase the food, and spend hours in the kitchen each Saturday and Sunday morning in preparation for the Sunday afternoon meal. I also direct clean-up after each meal. My menus are child friendly; I remove as much unnecessary fat and sugar as I can so the meal is both nutritious and delicious.

Among the favorite foods on the menu are the following:

- Deviled eggs
- Barbecued chicken
- Corn bread

---

3. Walker, "Teresa Flowers," *Beverly Citizen*.

- Mashed potatoes
- Banana pudding—Genny Peterson says that her favorite food on my menu is the banana pudding, hands down!
- Cakes baked with fruits and special flavoring inside

Happy relationships form and thrive among all those who lunch on my barbequed chicken, mashed potatoes, and deviled eggs! Youth Program Director Kari Marks captured the essence of the Pilgrim Church meal perfectly: "The smells of home cooking waft through the air as we fellowship together with praise teaching and prayer in the sanctuary. Our precious cook hovers at the kitchen door, apron on, surveying the crowd, knowing they will be fed both of soul and belly. The family is cared for well. All races, backgrounds, perspectives, and pocket sizes are welcome, and no one is the wiser. Its home and family, and you always know you are welcome, wanted, and loved."[4]

Pilgrim Church founders Pastor Jeff and Marjean Marks know that the lunches make people feel right at home: "Teresa's delicious meals bring a taste of home and family to the Pilgrim Church community. We all love to come to the table and celebrate Jesus, while enjoying those wonderful deviled eggs, mashed potatoes, and barbequed chicken that Teresa serves us. The memories of great food and Jesus' love unite us as a community in a wonderful way."[5]

Elder Jen Creamer explains why the lunches are so popular: "Where there is food, there is fellowship. The Community Meals Program not only provides lunch, but also facilitates the bonds of community as we take time to

4. Kari Marks, interview with author by email, June 2012.

5. Jeff and Marjean Marks, interview with author by email, June 2012.

Agape Feasts

get to know one another around the table. Many thanks are due to Teresa for her labor of love."[6] And Alice Shea sums up why the Pilgrim Church community meal, for her, is so compelling: "The church is people. Often times God brings me into contact with people through the Pilgrim Church community meal. People customarily gather around a meal. A person that you would not ordinarily share with will be open sharing a meal. Time must be made for friendship evangelism. It is an opportunity to find out about the faith of others. That is what community is: breaking bread with one another."[7]

Pilgrim Church represents several ethnic backgrounds. I am respectful of the cultural differences within the community and make my meals compatible to the tastes of our Nigerian, Haitian, Chinese, Korean, Creole, and Hispanic brothers and sisters.

Genny Peterson explains why people leave these lunches with smiles on their faces: "Some of the things that have made my heart fuzziest were seeing Teresa and others readily accommodate the nutritional or allergy needs of folks in the congregation. It's just so wise. Singing "happy birthday" to folks is always fun. And staying 'til two o' clock in the afternoon, on a regular basis, is certainly memorable as well."[8]

Maud Sandbo comments on the sensitivity to her dietary restrictions:

> I like the community meals much more than I thought I would—I found it a bit awkward at first, not knowing everybody, and having so many food allergies besides. I quickly felt right at home, however—it is like a real family meal,

---

6. Jen Creamer, interview with author by email, June 2012.
7. Alice Shea, interview with author in person, October 2012.
8. Genny Peterson, interview with author by email, June 2012.

Creative Ways to Build Christian Community

> in the best sense—low key, friendly, no fussing. I usually avoid situations where there is food because of my allergies which make it hard for me to eat meals with others, but at Pilgrim people are always trying to make sure that I have something good, too, so I'm not left hungry or left out of the circle. The love and fellowship is as nurturing as the food. It's been one of the most welcoming parts of getting to know Pilgrim Church.[9]

Jasmine Meyers adds,

> I remember when I first heard that Pilgrim Church regularly ate together, I thought, "Yes—that's what a church should be doing." I love standing in one of the oldest Christian traditions there is—breaking bread together. And Teresa Two Feathers takes such good care of me—I'm allergic to just about everything under the sun, and she always sets food aside specifically for me so that I'm not left out. I am so grateful for this sister of mine and her generous, giving spirit—I know the love she shows us is straight from the Lord."[10]

One of the delights of my life is the fact that Pilgrim Church's Costa Rican cherub, Carmen Trudeau, whips up salads in my kitchen and washes dishes with me. Carmen is witty, cute, and shares her spiritual insight generously in a wonderful Latin accent that is loaded with good humor and love. In her own words, Carmen sums what I feel about the lunch ministry: "Pilgrim Church Community Meal fulfills

---

9. Maud Sandbo, interview with author by email, June 2012.
10. Jasmine Meyers, interview with author by email, June 2012.

the purpose of Christian fellowship. It feeds the hungry food, and all those who take part in it are spiritually fed."[11]

HOW DOES THE PILGRIM CHURCH COMMUNITY MEALS PROGRAM BUILD COMMUNITY?

As Pastor Leslie McKinney's comments reveal, members of Pilgrim Church get to know each other over these home-cooked meals:

> Teresa's Sunday lunch ministry is one special way that Pilgrim Church builds community. We would never know each other the way we do, if we didn't sit down to share a meal together every month. This gives me an opportunity as pastor to know the hearts of the people at Pilgrim—to find out what's going on in their lives, to learn more about their jobs or school work, their family lives, personal struggles, travel experiences, and to know how to pray and minister more effectively. It's a beautiful gift that Teresa offers Pilgrim Church.[12]

Theodore Nelson describes the spiritual fellowship that the sharing of a community meal brings about: "With food comes fellowship. The breaking of natural bread is an appetizer for the spiritual bread which is the main course. Community gatherings with food, family, and friends are edifying, encouraging, and enjoyable."[13] And Gloria Wells observes, "I think the Pilgrim Church Community Meal

11. Carmen Trudeau, interview with author in person, June 2012.

12. Pastor Leslie McKinney, interview with author by email, June 2012.

13. Theodore Nelson, interview with author in person, October 2012.

Creative Ways to Build Christian Community

Program is great! It brings people in. When people see the love of God in Teresa as she prepares the meals, they respond. Jesus says that we need to take care of those in need."[14]

Valerie Crissman, Pilgrim Church Youth Pastor explains how hot lunches demonstrate Christian hospitality and give busy parents a break from cooking:

> The community meals at Pilgrim are times that I eagerly look forward to. Teresa often calls me in from doing "church work" to grab a plate and sit down. During this time, I not only check in with the teenagers with whom I serve, but I also have the "excuse" to talk with other adults in the church about life. Teresa always makes sure to tell my kids when she's serving their favorites, and I know that they love the meals to spend time with their church family. In addition, for many of our teens who rarely have family meals at home, I think Pilgrim shows them what love and community look like, particularly through this ministry of hospitality. Finally, I'm always thankful when we have a meal because it means if I have a meeting after church or my family has another engagement after church, I don't have to worry about what we will eat for lunch; it's all taken care of. I can't wait to see how God will continue to use the community meals at Pilgrim to show his love to our church and far beyond![15]

Douglas MacDougal appropriately describes the Pilgrim Church Community Meal as a time when Jesus builds the nerve endings of communication, sharing, and listening and the sinews of encouraging, inspiring, and healing. Such lunches bring non-Christians to the table with Christians

14. Gloria Wells, interview with author in person, October 2012.
15. Valerie Crissman, interview with author by email, June 2012.

Agape Feasts

and offer an informal and easy atmosphere for everyone. Linda Lockhart confirms his observations:

> At the beginning of my Christian life, a friend brought me to Pilgrim Church. Subsequent to my first visit to Pilgrim, I worked at Anchorage, a Beverly community residence for troubled boys, with Teresa Flowers. As a servant of the Lord, I can testify that Pilgrim Church Community Meals Program is a blessing because it brings many to the Lord's Table to sup who don't know Jesus. The Community Meal is an opportunity for those who don't know Jesus personally to feel His love and to experience His presence through fellowship.[16]

When people come to my luncheon table, they feel that love I have put into preparing their food. That love comes from Jesus. They eat my food and share the love of Jesus with one another. It is that simple. Genny Peterson, Gordon College graduate and Pilgrim Church member, explained that she believes in the power of mealtime to promote healthy relationships. She said that it was one of the things her mother strived for when she was young. In Genny's own words, "Sharing meals, that is, prepping them, eating them, and cleaning up after them, takes time, and all that equals love. And that's what we're about as folks who follow Jesus. This work happens naturally when you're sitting with folks. You figure it out. You have the TIME to."[17] Elder Curt Risley reveals the secret to the success of the lunch program: "Teresa's Sunday meals ministry builds community in this diverse congregation. This ministry is

---

16. Linda Lockhart, interview with author in person, May 2012.
17. Genny Peterson, interview with author by email, June 2012.

uncommon and is so important in making Pilgrim a different place to worship."[18]

It is so special to me that Michael Tornes credits the Pilgrim Community Meals program with changing his life. At my last lunch, Michael told me he thanked the Lord for the strength and motivation he received to better himself and expressed gratitude to Jesus for teaching him to keep faith in him: "One of the ways the Lord has taught me, motivated me, and strengthened me is through the Pilgrim Church Community Meal."[19] When Michael told me this, it meant so much as I understood his struggles and challenges.

Tanya Johnson gives Pilgrim Church credit for making a difference in her life at a difficult time: "I have always been the kind of person who would help people when they were down and out. It never occurred to me that I would be in a position of need. In a difficult time in the lives of my husband Dennis and me, Teresa Flowers and the Pilgrim Church housed me, fed me, and clothed me. Many thanks to you all. When I get back on my feet, I will make certain to help others in need."[20]

I love this beautiful poem that Jin Sook Kim wrote about our lunch program:

> We sit down to eat at Teresa's table;
> God connects our hearts together for love of Him and love of others.
> When we share each other's hearts and what is going on with each of us,
> our conversation goes deeper and deeper.
> We end up praying for each other.

---

18. Curt Risley, interview with author by email, June 2012.
19. Michael Tornes, interview with author in person, June 2012.
20. Tanya Johnson, interview with author in person, August 2012.

At Teresa's table, God brings people together, brings healing,
and brings safety, health, and love.
At Teresa's table, God redeems us in His love and comforts us in His Spirit
so that we can be victorious over an often chaotic, unloving, and discouraging world.
God uses Teresa to shine His light and His love on us.
God bless her.[21]

CONCLUSION

The Sunday meal preparation is hard work. But the effort is worth it as my life is blessed when I see solid Christian community built around my Sunday lunches. I want to thank each of my brothers and sisters who commented on the lunch program. It is a success because of my hard work and their participation. I am proud to be a descendant of the Cherokee nation. As a deacon and elder in Pilgrim Church, I want to encourage other Native American women to assume leadership in the church. In these challenging times, I hope that the Pilgrim Church Community Meals Program will inspire and encourage other Christian communities to organize community meals programs.

---

21. Poem submitted to be published in this chapter by Jin Sook Kim, July 2012.

3
The Arts: An Essential Dialogue for the Body of Christ
Olga Soler

IN GENESIS 1, THE Bible as we know it opens with God's lavish act of creation. In the same chapter we are told that human beings are created in the image of God (v. 26.) Why are we so afraid of creativity? It is part of the image we were created into. We need to remember that God is not only a precise and exact scientist but also a prodigious and sumptuous artist. The extent of his innovation knows no bounds.

WE LOVE IT; WE HATE IT

The church has had a long standing love/hate relationship with the arts. There have been many times when the people of God have put art down as idolatry, minimized it as unessential, or strangled and stifled it as unimportant, or even forbidden it. Those of us who are Gen Xers can remember the controversy over rock and roll and drums in the church, and many a modern artist of the 1970s remembers being ostracized for our abstract offerings. These are moot points since rock is now common transcultural coinage, and many churches have a trap set on the podium and a sound system that matches the Orpheum Theatre's—but we learned, didn't we? If we want any young people in the church or if

The Arts: An Essential Dialogue for the Body of Christ

we want to relate to those in the present culture at all—in other words, if we want to build community—we have to bend. Try as it might, the church cannot live without the arts nor was it meant to.

At times, however, powerful factions in the church have found the arts too difficult to control, and so they have attempted to marginalize them and the artists with them. Why does this happen? Some say that the answer lies in the right and left brain dilemma. Those who are left-brained, linear thinkers are less apt to see the usefulness of art and may even feel threatened by it. Those who are right-brained, divergent thinkers can't live without it. Behavioral scientists say that, like east and west, these two kinds of people will always be polar opposites and unable to agree.[1] The body of Christ, however, does not have the luxury of saying that the left or the right-brained thinkers can be done away with. These are our brothers and sisters, and the Lord wants us to get along. In him and with love we will find our common ground. When freedom in the Spirit is allowed with the proper biblical precautions—"Quench not the Spirit. Despise not prophesyings. Prove all things; hold fast that which is good. Abstain from all appearance of evil" (1 Thess 5:19–22 KJV)—the arts proliferate and enrich the life of the body without question. They also attract others to the fold.

IS ART BIBLICAL?

Where is art in the Bible? Everywhere. From the music of Jubal to the dances of Miriam, it is there. Ezekiel portrayed his prophecies dramatically, with staging and props as directed by God. The Tabernacle itself and all its services were a daily drama portraying the story of our salvation. We also

1. Mooney, "Brain"; Haidt, *Righteous Mind*.

see the prophets from Samuel's time playing music as they prophesied, and when Saul joined in their prophesying it was said of him, "Is Saul also among the prophets?"(1 Sam 10:11 NIV). In Masoretic texts of the Hebrew Scriptures, musical notations were placed all through the words along with the vowel pointings. These were known as *te'amim* or *cantillation* marks used to sing the scriptures. The Jews still use a similar system today.[2] Sculpture which has come under fire because of fear of idolatry was also acceptable as long as one did not bow down to it as an object of worship, and we see sculpture in the Tabernacle as well as the Temple. David, the king, had a choir and orchestra ready twenty-four hours a day for worship (1 Chr 9:33). Some of them were said to prophesy by music. Elisha once asked for a minstrel to play music so that he might prophesy (2 Kgs 3:15). We also find that the craftsmen who fashioned the Tabernacle and all its utensils were not just inspired, but were "moved" by the Spirit to do their works, as were the prophets. One can scarcely think of the Old Testament without observing the ubiquitous presence of art. In the New Testament, Jesus followed the tradition of the Rabbis in teaching through storytelling (parables). From cover to cover we see art.

THE SCRUTINY OF ART

So, why is art questioned or even thought of as "alternative" ministry when it has such a strong biblical foundation? If one was not influenced by overly conservative thinking, one would be more inclined to consider art an essential part of telling the story of the Bible, of worshipping, and

2. British & Foreign Bible Society, "The Masoretes"; see also these Web sites: http://www.lrz.de/~hr/teamim/; http://en.wikipedia.org/wiki/Hebrew_punctuation.

of ministering the gospel to a fallen world. In Medieval times, plays were used by the guilds to tell Bible stories to the largely illiterate population. During the Renaissance, art told Christ's story everywhere in painting and sculpture. Among the romantics, the impressionists, and the realists we find offerings to the glory of God. I stood in a church near Kent, England, where the stained glass windows had been designed by the Jewish artist Marc Chagall. The windows were designed in honor of the daughter of the Jewish family who owned the property and still allowed Christians to worship there. They had lost a daughter to drowning. In the main window, Jesus is depicted on the cross looking down on the suffering of the family at the death of the innocent girl: ready to receive her into paradise. It showed that Jew and Gentile could be together in beauty, light, and grace.

CULTURALLY CORRECT

African-American Gospel music, as well as Beethoven and Vivaldi, has reached the heights with sacred music. As a result, many people who would not attend a cathedral have been swept away to a place where they unknowingly desire to go by the Spirit who inspired these melodious strains. World music, that is, music from native peoples around the world, can also praise God. When we say that only an organ and not a drum or a didgeridoo (a native Australian instrument) is fit for worship, we needlessly alienate those to whom this auditory genre speaks. An organ can be sinful and a drum sacred, or vice versa, depending on the heart of the player. We need to get that straight and stop making cultural judgments where expression is concerned.

Creative Ways to Build Christian Community

PREACHING IS AN ART, BUT NOT THE ONLY ONE

Preaching, or oratory, itself is a kind of art, but it is not the only one. To say that preaching is the most important art form is to allow many of the other gifts in the body to atrophy. Preaching in our media and sound-bite oriented society is very limited in its ability to speak to the common culture. Educators everywhere are discovering that, unless students participate, have something to look at, or some music to accompany a message, for the most part, that message is simply not reaching the targeted audience. Of course even a donkey can be used by God to bring his message, but that again highlights the versatility of God. He can use many things to reach us, not just words spoken by one person.

Art can be, but is not necessarily, a mere accessory to the spoken message. The thought of using art to "dress up" a message irks me as a serious artist. It feels like cheap advertising. On the other hand, the idea of portraying a message is exciting, and I have never seen art fail to reach its audience on some deep and personal level. I had an art center at which we staged multimedia events with themes like "storms," "clean comedy," "martyrdom," "transparency," etc. Each event had interactive, graphic, musical, and dramatic components. People came and were entertained and challenged, and they participated. Each event had a strong spiritual message that was clearly Christian. Non-believers attended each event and were always intrigued as well as delighted. We even had one event wherein we requested that no non-believers attend because we felt it was too cryptic for people who were not yet in the faith. A non-believer got in anyway and enjoyed it thoroughly.

The Arts: An Essential Dialogue for the Body of Christ

In the United Kingdom, I was part of a Christian organic community for two years. We did not have to do anything to attract people. They were curious about us. Besides ministry-related work, we also farmed and sold vegetables to the surrounding hotels. God worked to give us many opportunities to interact with the people around us. Many of us were artists and musicians, so one way we held converse with our neighbors was to have concerts at our large house every Friday. Many people came and enjoyed the music. A lot of people got the message; we saw many saved. Our band also went down to the local pubs quite frequently and played our music there. We never drank, but (by request) played lots of rounds of "Amazing Grace." The unmistakable message and the unforgettable tune still speak even to worldly crowds, do they not?

Over the years, I have traveled with several dramatic groups for whom I wrote and directed. We never did a performance without coming away with a testimony. People poured their drugs down the toilet and gave their hearts to Christ. We saw healings of cancer and healings of marriages. It was work, but, when the Spirit speaks through whatever medium he chooses, it never fails to hit the mark. I also traveled across the United States and the United Kingdom on my own teaching on addiction, recovery from abuse, and biblical themes. I used all of the arts to illustrate my work and had doctors asking me questions and using me as a consultant. I did conference workshops that brought hope to hundreds of people through therapeutic dance, drama, and comedy. My arts-based recovery group (Discovery) was voted most encouraging and enlightening by the clients at the Boston Rescue Mission.

Creative Ways to Build Christian Community

MAKING LASTING IMPRESSIONS

People remember very little of what we say, but an image or a presentation that draws in an audience burns itself into the soul on many sensory levels. At a coffee house, I once performed my version of the "Red Dancing Shoes" to illustrate addiction, anger, and redemption. I wasn't sure if the colorful population in the audience was getting it, but I did my best and left the rest to God. Two months later, I was at the coffee house again, this time in the audience. A kind of scary, tall woman with heavy makeup, bleached hair, high-heeled boots, and lots of chains came up to me. She pointed her long, red fingernail right at me and said, "YOU!" I winced, hoping she was not mistaking me for someone who owed her money. She continued, "You was here a couple of months ago, and you did this thing, this thing with the red shoes . . . I was moved, very moved." Whew, was I relieved. I was also glad that what I had portrayed did something good for this woman who could barely describe what she had seen. The point is that a holy impression was made. She came back to the coffee house because the message spoke to her on a level she was able to internalize and understand.

THE NEUTRALITY OF ART

The language of art is a spiritual one. Yes, it can be dark or even evil spiritually speaking, but it is a *neutral medium* that bends to the artist who uses it. It was originally intended to be good, and it can still be a power for good. Art accesses the part of our consciousness where our wonder, pain, intuition, and pleasure live. It draws us to itself and reaches us subconsciously before we even have time to think about what we are experiencing. Art can be used to heal, to teach, to enjoy, and to challenge. It can make you smile and swoon, and it can make you mad. In Deuteronomy 6:5, we are told that our relationship to God needs to be one that includes all our heart, soul, and strength. From this we can deduce that belief of a merely intellectual nature is not as desirable as faith born in the heart. The heart cannot be told; it must be inspired. We must, therefore, learn to speak the heart's language. The language of the heart is that of spirit, symbol, and emotion. Data comes to us through the mind but saving faith through the heart. We need information, but it will never save us. Art specializes in teaching us in the core of our consciousness. This is not to promote sickly sentimentality or a belief based on how we feel. The language of our feeling, memories, dreams, and hopes is best portrayed by art. That is why God uses it so much in his word and why he uses it so powerfully still.

IT CAN HELP US TO BELIEVE

I attended a conference at which a portrayal of heaven was being dramatized. In the audience, a young woman who had been in a wheelchair for two years was watching. She saw people coming to Jesus at the pearly gates and throwing crutches away as well as receiving sight and health of all kinds. She was so moved that she stood up and walked to the front herself; of course, that stopped the show. What was portrayed had become reality because the kingdom of God is with us now as well as when we are brought to glory. Let this message come any way the Spirit chooses to bring it. "No eye has seen, no ear has heard, no mind has conceived what God has prepared for those who love him" (1 Cor 2:9 NIV). Art can help us see, to a degree, that which is hard to conceive. Of course, we will not even have time to talk about literature and film, but in your fellowship you may well have budding or hidden screenwriters and authors, producers, and directors. C.S. Lewis, George McDonald, and J.R.R. Tolkien's voices still speak even on the big screen. Thank the Lord they spoke forth as they did when many thought they were silly or too fanciful.

Changes inspired by art have also impacted people who believe. This has taken place many times and in startling ways at our presentations. Once a woman came up to me after a performance; she was ashen and drawn. She looked like she was dying or drugged. According to what she told me, she had been this way for years. I answered her questions about what she had seen, a presentation about our power of choice as people of God. Time passed, and months later the same woman approached me after a performance. I could not recognize her as the same woman. She looked radiant. When I asked her what made the difference, she said, "You showed me with your play that I was not trapped. I had choices, and I made them for the good."

Another man saw a presentation I did on children and family. I remember it was a really fun night with lots of kids. There was a lot of comedy, but the message was loud and clear: children are important, and they are only children for a short time. I saw the man again four years later. He approached me and told me how he had been convicted that night to spend more time with his children. He had even changed his job so that he could do that because the job he had previously took him away from his family so much. He was so happy he had made the change, and so were his wife and children. He had heard lots of sermons on similar subjects, but the show made a profound enough impression on him to drive him to change. I could go on and on with other similar stories.

The Arts: An Essential Dialogue for the Body of Christ

TEAM OF DREAMS

Another benefit of the artistic process in the church is unity. Doing a project as a group stretches us and builds us up as a team. We all have to move as one to accomplish the goal—and isn't that what being the body of Christ is all about? When you are in a choir or a band, or doing a mural together or an installation or a play, you learn about yourself and you learn about the people with you. You pull together, and the result is beautiful and meaningful. It is not like a sport where one team wins and the other loses or where you have nothing but bruises at the end. When you are finished, you have a product that you can be proud of. You have something that speaks. It is like doing a sermon as an ensemble: one person does not take the credit, but the credit goes to God. It is a humbling experience because you know you could not have accomplished it alone. It reminds me of the building of the Tabernacle. When Moses asked the people to contribute, they brought so much material, money, and talent that he finally had to tell them to stop giving. Everyone wanted to participate. What an ensemble piece that was.

One of the groups I was in did a play about suicide in the church. The play was written after the suicide of a prominent church member whom everyone thought was the most perfect woman. Her appearance and deportment were flawless, but she had a terrible secret which caused her much pain, and she did not feel that she could share it with anyone. We did not want this kind of thing to happen again. We wanted to help churches create the kind of fellowship that would be safe for a person to unload such burdens so that they could be carried to the Lord and healed. So with this script the cast became a prophetic force, and we saw wonderful changes in people both in the cast and outside of it as we performed. Of course the enemy was not pleased with this, and so we encountered quite a bit of spiritual resistance, but this galvanized us to persevere and to stay united in our cause. I don't think any of us will forget the experience. I know this play saved lives. Art is not a game. It can be fun, but it is also a serious spiritual exercise that brings about gut-level reactions. When I was a young believer, an old veteran of the faith looked at me and said, "Remember, when the word of God is proclaimed in Spirit and in truth you will see a riot or a revival." I know now what he meant.

THE ELEMENT OF SURPRISE

Art can take you by surprise. I remember an all-day gospel event outside of the Boston Aquarium. Many churches were there participating in music and preaching. We saw a lot of people going by, but few stopping to listen. This was a bit frustrating. I was to do a presentation of the "Prodigal Son" in dance drama and song. My choreography called for me to be on the floor at times. To my dismay when I went up to the area where I was to dance I found that it was covered with broken glass. I had prayed, and I knew that I did not have time to deliberate or to clear my set. So I just started in and did my dance as planned with minor modifications to avoid the debris. As I executed the moves, I could see that people were stopping. They were riveted. People put their books, newspapers, and electronic devices aside to watch. God had their attention. The glass might have added to the affect.

Another time we went to perform on a town common, and to our dismay we found that there was a Hare Krishna convention right near us. As we got up to perform, a crowd formed to watch us: business people, bikers, and young lovers. We had a good crowd, but now the Hare Krishnas were parading behind us in all their regalia with a thirty-foot idol covered in diaphanous saffron material. We thought we would lose the crowd. Some heads turned, but the power of the portrayed story and dance anointed with the Spirit of God was stronger. We did not lose anyone; Jesus got through.

THE HUMAN ELEMENT

There is something about art that deeply connects with humans. Once I performed the "Prodigal Son" for a group of hardened addicts and street people. A man came to me afterward and said, "I know I have hurt my grandfather the way that boy hurt his dad. I need to call him and tell him I'm sorry." What a victory that was. If we don't keep the attention of the people, then what good is the message? Stories keep people's attention. That is why the art of storytelling and portraying will never lose its power even in a society jaded by special effects and celluloid hype. Jesus told stories, and we need to do so as well. I thought I had reached the attention limit of a crowd of teenagers once with a story I acted out for them. To my surprise, when I told them it was almost done, they asked for more. Just like little ones, they wanted another and another. Storytelling is a powerful art.

The art of mime needs no translation; it connects without words and can be understood in any language. It is hard to ignore a mime and even harder to argue with one. Mime is a great vehicle for the gospel. I once did a mime presentation for a group of survivors of abuse. The presentation was about coming out of the silence and how God waits for us and gives us a voice. When the message was over, no one in the audience of about three hundred people applauded. I was quite taken by the anointing that I felt, so I did not question the reaction. I just started to walk off the platform; then I heard sobs from all over the audience. People were weeping everywhere. One woman collapsed and had to be taken out by a counselor. This had a very good outcome toward her breakthrough I was told. It was the greatest compliment I ever received as a performer.

ART AND THE PROPHETIC

They are not always the same thing, but art and prophecy walk a similar path. To prophesy is to speak, sing, act, or dance (move) by inspiration of a spirit. Worldly people call it having a muse; we call it following God's lead. Our "muse" is Christ. There is good prophesying and bad, as you know—probably because there is the Holy Spirit and bad spirits doing the inspiring. When the Spirit of the Lord inspires someone, people called it being anointed or inspired, as with Bezalel and Oholiab the artisans of the Tabernacle, or David when he played the harp that soothed Saul's madness. People who are afraid of art are often also afraid of or skeptical about miracles, healings, prophetic words, and other manifestations of the Spirit. All of these things are gifts from the Lord. Poor is the church that puts them in the closet or on the shelf because of skepticism, unbelief, or fear. At present, many believing artists are learning to wait on the Lord for holy improvisation (inspiration in motion) from the Lord: We are learning to make music in the moment. We are learning to receive the story God may give us at any given time to minister to a person or people we may not even know. This includes dancing war dances against illness, evil, or darkness wherever we may be asked to do it, even if we have never done it before. In doing these things at the bidding of the Lord, unrehearsed and unexpected, we are finding great things are being accomplished in a moment. If improvisation is a challenge for the unbeliever, it is a delight for the believer because we take our orders from the Lord and so join in a great adventure with him.

INVITING ART IN

If at this point you are sold on exploring the possibilities of art, how do you invite it back into the church? It is very simple. Set the artists free. Trust them; make room for them. Let them be themselves, participate with them. Encourage them to listen to what God is saying to them and allow them to present it with the talent he has given to them. Confess past rigidity and control. Banish fear and trust in what the Spirit wants to do with the talents of every person—not just the preachers and teachers. Many people are sitting in pews vegetating because they are not given the opportunity to do what they do best. Moreover, many are beginning to realize that church was not always what it is now.

A LIVING CHURCH

There was a time in the beginning of the body of Christ (and for three hundred years after it began) that preaching was used mainly for evangelism, and fellowship consisted mostly of people ministering to one another with their gifts and in the breaking of bread and communion.[3] It was understood by every believer that the church was not a building, but that the people were the church. Every member was expected to bring something in the Spirit to the table of fellowship. (See 1 Corinthians 14.) If you ask me, that organic way of doing church is the best. Is it any wonder

3. Viola and Barna, *Pagan Christianity*, 85.

that growth was unparalleled in the early church? It can be that way again.

Having been a participant in organic and creative ministry for many years, I know very well how attractive and exciting it is. We do not have to sell it because it attracts people all on its own. If the Holy Spirit is leading, church is always surprising and new every day. People like that. They are drawn to it. Creative, personal, Christ-centered, organic (or living) fellowship is a magnet because it speaks to people in a language that all can comprehend on some level. It also gives people what they really need. People are church-phobic these days. There are many reasons for this, and not all of these are the fault of outsiders. Our "Christianese" has to be translated for them; it is foreign to their ears. Art can bridge the communication gap in many ways. Genuine, transparent, and loving fellowship in the Spirit can do the rest.

DO THEY GET IT?

We had a techno event at the arts place one night that was a great example of these points. It was the night before Easter Sunday, and we wanted to do a resurrection theme. Our theater had all black walls and an all black ceiling, as many theaters do. We placed a slab on a desk and put it on the stage. We placed ultraviolet lights everywhere. The music started. As people came in, we asked them to take some chalk and draw their idea of angels on the walls. These were illuminated by the black light, giving them an "otherworldly" effect. We had other people working on a mural which depicted the opening of a cave with a view of the dawn in it. We lit the installation so that the light appeared to be entering in from outside the cave. An installation is a sculpture that takes up a whole area, sort of like an artistic biosphere. On the slab we had other people "building" a man. They stuffed clothes till we had the shape of a man and then wound bandages around him. The bandages were of a white shiny material that caught the light nicely. After we wound him like a mummy, we took the tail of all the bandages and draped them over the pipes on the ceiling. It gave them the appearance of floating in the air, as if they were coming off of the body by themselves. We then strewed red roses all over the installation, and along with the "floating" bandages we had chains that were also sort of floating off of the body.

The people did not know what they were doing or why, but those of us who were believers had the opportunity to speak to them a little here and there as we worked. We were instructed not to talk too much. The piece spoke for itself. We called it "moments before dawn on the 1st day." The dead man was, of course, Christ, and the bandages and chains were falling off of him because death was leaving him as the resurrection began to take place. The roses were symbols of the love that made it all possible. When it was all over, everyone found themselves in the middle of the tomb with Christ about to rise from the dead. The anticipation was palpable. Was this all too weird for people to understand? We heard one "not yet believing" girl remark as she stared at the finished work, "Oh poor, poor Jesus!" The message was obviously hitting the mark with her and with others. Then we celebrated and danced with angels all around, and we all had a great time.

The world accuses believers of being uptight and repressed. Intuitively, like animals, they can smell the fear on us. We are so afraid of doing the wrong thing that we are paralyzed instead of living. We fear so much, forgetting that fear of God is the only thing we really need to worry about (Matt 10:28); otherwise, fear is the devil's domain. The Lord tells us to "fear not." Our God is Creator, and we are made in his image. We need not be limited to one or two methods or programs of worshipping him, giving him glory, or spreading his word. The Lord made each of us unique individuals, and he has a unique way to reach each person he made. There is no "one size fits all" way to serve those around us or to communicate with them about what is important. If we remain unafraid and flexible, God will surprise all of us with millions of ways to reach out. Creativity is unbounded and needs only have the limits love places upon it.

OUR BROTHER AND SISTER ARTISTS

There are many reasons why people leave the church. Many of them do not have to do with Christ. The main reason why artists leave is that they feel stifled or distrusted simply because they are different or do not behave according to the status quo. I attended a concert a few years ago. The genre of the music was heavy metal, and the musicians were unbelievably talented. The lead guitarist began to play a piece called "For the Love of God," and I witnessed the most amazing portrayal of worship I have ever seen. This man fairly writhed with the tender and fervent emotion of devotion. Nothing he did that evening would lead me to believe he was not a sincere or decent person. He might even have been a believer, and the reaction from the audience was one of awe and contemplation. I don't know if he professed Christ, but we should all come to Jesus with such verve. Now, before anyone judges me for this sentiment, I would caution you to remember the story of Michal, King David's wife, who criticized her husband for dancing his love and praise to the Lord. She was punished for that and ended up barren. Will the church experience something similar if it rejects the arts? Fruitfulness too is part of our creativity. Let us instead banish fear and bring forth all that God would create through us.

4

A Listening Heart

Cathy Squires

On the day of her 40th wedding anniversary, a colleague of mine in the early childhood mental health field said she was so glad that she had remained married to her husband, because it had taken her 40 years to learn what it meant to love another person. When I think about the development of Christian community between two persons or among a group of people, I think of it as having elements of a long marriage, a journey of learning to live and learning to love oneself and to love another. It is a long, slow journey to enter more and more into the love relationship among the Godhead: Father, Son, and Holy Spirit. We learn to trust and to receive the Triune God's love for humanity. We learn to turn around and share this love with others. It is a journey of healing and of reclaiming the missing pieces of our rightful inheritance as God's beloved children.

My first experience of Christian community with a group was with the Christian World Liberation Front (CWLF) in Berkeley, California. CWLF was birthed as an outreach to the counterculture—a hand extended to those who wanted to drop out of the "establishment" (the cultural mainstream) for one reason or another. It seemed to me that, for some, it was just an excuse for prolonging their

A Listening Heart

adolescence; for others, it was a time of serious values clarification. People in CWLF fell between these two poles.

It was through a friend's invitation to a CWLF Bible study (called the Monday Night Bible Rap in the Berkeley lingo) that I soon became part of this community. I was born in Calcutta, India, to Chinese parents and grew up in Hong Kong; I immigrated to the United States in 1967 to pursue higher education. In my early 20s I found myself at the University of California, Berkeley, eager to break away from home to find my own values and to become my own person.

One thing that really attracted me to CWLF was the diversity of people in it. There were outstanding thinkers with their advanced degrees living alongside high school/college drop-outs, "acid heads," and "mental cases" relating to each other as equals. What made this possible was the freedom in the community to be who you were and to speak truth. Those who thrived in CWLF were people who had a sense of humor and didn't take themselves too seriously. I was curious, enthusiastic, dedicated, and full of youthful idealism. I felt that love could conquer all and could bring any two persons or groups together. What would the Good News be about if that were not true?

Based on that premise, with my own cultural and family background, my personality makeup, and what was happening around me, I worked tirelessly to relate to anyone who came into the community. My view of the Christian community as family made me look for a relational structure as well (the Chinese family has elaborately prescribed roles for a functioning relational system). Relating to people who were so different from me meant a lot of intense and reflective listening. There were many things that did not immediately make sense to me, but I was not willing to make snap judgments or come to hasty conclusions. I learned to listen to myself and others as I constantly mulled things over.

Some time after my involvement in the community, my working relationship and friendship with Bill Squires, a Caucasian CWLF campus worker, evolved into a dating relationship. By that time, I was in my senior year. One day, a community member nicknamed Small Paul asked me, "How does it feel to be dating a national handball champion?" I mumbled something like, "I don't feel anything," or "What is there to feel something about?" I could not find words to tell him that, according to my cultural upbringing, playing ball was for those who were not suited for scholarly pursuits, for academic success. As a result of this deep-seated attitude, even today, athletic trainers in China go to the countryside to look for potential Olympic competitors among the poor and uneducated. This is seen as a way for the poor to have an opportunity to climb out of poverty since academia is beyond their grasp. How could I feel pride then that my boyfriend was a sports champion? This is one example of how I had to work hard to sort through my own thinking and feelings as I lived in the CWLF community.

On June 12th, 1971, Bill and I married. It was the third interracial marriage in my family, and so it did not create any large waves. In the most basic Christian community unit, our marriage, I could sometimes feel the richness and sometimes the challenges of a cross-cultural relationship. I continued to realize over and over again that true deep listening is a skill and grace that one has to cultivate and grow in.

Loyalty to family was one of my deeply held cultural values, one which I maintained as I treated the church community as family. I soon transferred all my deeply held values to the community of CWLF. I held the leaders and my husband in esteem and served them devotedly. No task

A Listening Heart

was beneath me because I was serving a great cause and a great community. Even though I cannot now locate the article, I remember agreeing with an author who said that no matter how much American researchers study the secrets of the success of Japanese business management, and try to transfer these principles to the United States, the transfer is doomed to failure because the American culture cannot duplicate centuries of cultural mores that cause a janitor at Mitsubishi to say with deep pride, "I work for Mitsubishi." In the same way, I derived much of my identity from being a member of CWLF.

My time with the community of CWLF and, later, my four years with the House Church of Berkeley exposed me to many classes, programs, interactions, and conversations with creative and free thinkers. I had many opportunities to embark on a journey of deeper discovery of myself, others, the world, and God.

One significant subject we all considered was the role of women in ministry and in leadership. Egalitarianism in marriage was supported. I also pondered subjects related to the perils of professionalism, psychotherapy in cultural perspective (my undergraduate degree was in psychology), energy conservation, simple living, regard for the poor, and other global concerns.

In those days, some of the books circulating in our midst were:

- *Living Together in A World Falling Apart* by Dave and Neta Jackson
- *Small Is Beautiful* by E. F. Schumacher
- *Diet for a Small Planet* by Frances Moore Lappe
- *All We're Meant To Be* by Letha Scanzoni and Nancy Hardesty
- *Call to Commitment* by Elizabeth O'Connor

Creative Ways to Build Christian Community

- *Let Justice Roll Down* by John Perkins
- *Life Together* by Dietrich Bonhoeffer

The ponderings of those days formed some core values that have remained with me until today.

After six wonderful years, our close-knit CWLF community went through a split. It broke into two (and then later three) communities: Redeemer King Church, House Church of Berkeley, and Bartimaeus Community. The pain and challenge of these agonizing schisms led me to deep personal, life, value, and theological reflections. The intensity of interactions and the depth of relationships made these splits a source of deep pain and disillusionment. The cultural difference of individualism and group loyalty, at work with my personality makeup, plunged me into grief from loss and a measure of identity diffusion. I wondered what good opening my home and my heart had really done. I wondered if I had been foolish in giving myself so wholeheartedly to "these people." I purposed to be more circumspect in trusting/respecting others, and in developing friendships. I wanted a less intentional and intense community so that I could rest, heal, and "just be."

And "just be" is what I did in the ensuing years at the Berkeley Covenant Church! I felt I was being self-protective, conservative, and doing only what came "naturally" to me. The sermons I heard, the manner in which I was pastored, and the growth opportunities provided were just what I needed. A group of us in the church, including myself, went through the Spiritual Exercises of Ignatius of Loyola with the pastors. I had the opportunity to receive Spiritual Direction from one of the pastors when I went through a rough patch in guiding my children through the life passage of adolescence. I did much "traveling in," and "traveling down" with Christ. I remember exclaiming in one of

A Listening Heart

the Berkeley Covenant Church Sunday School classes that I had to enter my Asian and personal hell before I could rise with Christ in his resurrection.

I was far from being idle during this time. I gathered a wonderful staff-team to operate and expand the church-owned preschool, led the church in a building project that housed a residence and two large preschool classrooms, and did a few other things on the side. Even though a lot of people around me felt that I was a risk-taker and engaged in "thinking outside of the box," I was just comfortably being myself. I often reflected on the fact that my work was so much my creative self-expression that it was hard for me to tell whether it was my work or my play. Our staff team often included some of society's unlikely people.

I was feeling very comfortable in my leadership at the Berkeley Covenant Church, not "involv[ing] myself in great matters, or in things too difficult for me" (Ps 131:1 NASB). My relationship with the triune God was slowly deepening. God's word became alive to me. For example, the following passage significantly ministered to me: "I, the Lord, am your God, who brought you up from the land of Egypt; open your mouth wide and I will fill it . . . . with honey from the rock I would satisfy you" (Ps 81:10, 16 NASB). In my healing, freedom, and rest, I began to have a sense that God's call on my life was in one way or another to cooperate with God "to proclaim release to the captives and recovery of sight to the blind, to set free those who are oppressed . . . " (Luke 4:18 NASB).

In this atmosphere of rest, freedom, and a continual desire for growth and change, I decided to enroll in a Master's Program in Pastoral Counseling at Holy Names University. What attracted me to this particular program was that it was designed for people who had full-time jobs and also that it gave multiple opportunities to reach one's own goal and stop. A person can do 12 units to get a certificate in Pastoral Counseling or continue on to get a MA in Pastoral Counseling or carry on further to qualify to sit for the Marriage and Family Therapist track. It felt like a safe and conservative path for a person with family and work responsibilities.

During all these years, the vision of a local church as people sharing life together never left me. In fact, my Masters' thesis was on the church as a therapeutic community. I argued that a properly functioning Christian community ought to give ample opportunities for people in it to grow past many of their dysfunctions as they relate to each other with truth, forgiveness, and love.

Imagine my reluctance as well as excitement when God began to call me to leave this comfortable place to help plant a church in the inner city in East Oakland where Bill had been doing youth work for about 15 years. I could not understand why God would not call somebody else more suited to the job, someone more extroverted, someone with more leadership abilities, and someone with more of everything. God gently coaxed me into surrendering to his promptings. I decided to take the plunge and to influence young people not to make the mistakes I had made as a youthful idealist in Berkeley. I sought to be as faithful to God and to his call as I could. Many times it felt like a second round of the diverse CWLF community to me: mainstream, poor, wounded, and misfits.

In the larger perspective of my story, it was a time of consolidating all of my life experiences up to 1995. These experiences would help me to cooperate with God in what He wanted to do in this East Oakland neighborhood in terms of creating a specific local worshipping community. I had learned a lesson I needed to continue to learn throughout

A Listening Heart

my life with God: how to relinquish control, get myself out of the way, and allow God to do whatever he wants.

In the course of focusing on empowering neighborhood people, especially the 1.5 immigrant generation (those who were minors when they immigrated), I realized that I was groping for some additional tools that would enable deeply wounded people (and that seems to be most of us) to make choices that would create more stability in their/our lives. It seemed like God heard my cry when I stumbled upon the Life Skills International curriculum.

Life Skills International was founded by Paul and Judy Hegstrom and grew out of their own life history of being respectively perpetrator and victim of domestic violence. The Life Skills curriculum seemed concise, comprehensive, and understandable to a broad audience. It was like putting cookies on a lower shelf for everyone to reach. It was especially important to me that it made sense to people who were either perpetrators or victims of violence.

Bill and I felt that it was an appropriate tool for the vision we were given for the Oakland church plant and beyond. It is a great curriculum to help people deal with childhood wounds that get in the way of adult functioning. We realized that, as the interior noise created by childhood wounds subsided, people could hear themselves and others more clearly. But, most importantly, people could hear God more clearly. When the power of the subconscious mind begins to lose its grip on a person, he or she can then make healthier, more informed, and positive choices. I felt led to devote my energy to the facilitating of this curriculum, and to a ministry of prayer, listening, and healing, including the ancient practice of Spiritual Direction.

In the current economic downturn, with housing prices slipping to an all-time low, God opened up the door for us to purchase a small house next door to our residence

Creative Ways to Build Christian Community

in West Sacramento. Our vision is to devote it to short-term retreats for people, especially people in ministry who sometimes find themselves in great need of rest and spiritual refreshing but are financially depleted. Some may need deep healing. Located in a poor, heavily Hispanic neighborhood, we named it Casa Perla to signify the desire for God that visitors will bring with them: a search for the Pearl of Great Price (Matt 13:46). We hope to gather a team of people interested to work alongside us to minister to weary ones.

As I reflect on my journey in hospitality of heart and home, I realize that God has been the constant host and companion. God's grace and mercy hover over me and invite me to his banqueting table. My response to the invitation need not be judged; I merely need to follow with all of my heart. I may stumble and fall, but it is God who picks me up. When two persons asked Jesus where he was staying (John 1:38–39), he said to them, "Come and see." They followed and stayed the night. Never mind whether we said "Yes" to God out of desperation, out of curiosity, out of a sense of heroism, out of who knows what lies in the depth of us. If we want God in any way, God will journey with us to our death. As we enter into death with Jesus, we will also rise with Jesus in his resurrection. Our cleansing from sin allows us fellowship with God and with each other, making community possible.

We thank God that even though we have made lots of mistakes in life, God has made us resilient and creative. We pray that in rest and healing, guests will enter ever more deeply into their true selves, become part of true communities, where all forms of idolatries are put away, and worship God in spirit and in truth.

As I reflect on the twists and turns of my life, the highs and lows, I have come to some understanding of God's promise in 2 Corinthians 12:9: "My grace is sufficient for you, for power is perfected in weakness" (NASB). As I live life with Abba Father as God's much-loved child, I have also come to understand some of what Paul said in 1 Corinthians 4:3, when he wrote, "I do not even judge myself" (NIV). Community is found in the absence of judgment and in the presence of deep listening to God. Deep listening to God leads to discernment and to compassionate action. Community is sometimes discovered in surprising settings. Blessed are those who find these settings—they are precious gifts from God.

5
A Look at New Beginnings
Jeff Marks

INTRODUCTION

IN THIS CHAPTER I will focus on the relational aspects of communal prayer. I will do this by sharing my personal experience with it. For forty years, I have traveled and interceded in prayer with thousands of Christians worldwide. As a result, a very distinct Christian network has developed. This community is one of the most joyous benefits of global intercessory prayer movement.

I will begin by describing several startup communities that I was involved in. These ministries model highly creative ways to build Christian community. The first was the Bronxville Christian Fellowship, which was located just outside the city limits of New York City. The second was the Beverly Christian Fellowship. This was a fellowship plant in Beverly, Massachusetts of the Bronxville Christian Fellowship in New York. The reason I use the term *fellowship* and not *church* is because these bodies of Christ specifically model Christian community; some churches have community and some don't. The Beverly Christian Fellowship merged into what is now the Pilgrim Church of Beverly MA.

A Look at New Beginnings

THE BRONXVILLE CHRISTIAN FELLOWSHIP

The Bronxville Fellowship was non-denominational and multi-ethnic. My wife, Marjean, and I began this fellowship when we visited her parents in Bronxville, New York for Thanksgiving in 1971. We continued our previous ministry commitments going back and forth between Dartmouth College and the University of Virginia while we started the Bronxville Fellowship. Marjean and I saw many miracles at the Dartmouth College and the University of Virginia ministries, and we planned to continue with these ministries. To our surprise, the Holy Spirit would not let us leave Bronxville, so we waited on the Lord and prayed. An *au pair,* named Ingelise, from Denmark, came to work for my mother-in-law at that time. Marjean and I led her quickly to the Lord. Sometime after that, I met a veteran who just returned from Vietnam and was wearing a cast. He had stepped on a land mine in Vietnam. His leg was filled with shrapnel, and he had osteomyelitis, which is an incurable bone disease. He accepted the Lord and was healed during our time at the Bronxville Fellowship. He and Ingelise married and became the core of the Bronxville Fellowship.

My mother-in-law suggested that we start meetings in her spacious living room on Wednesday nights. The room quickly filled with teenagers and au pairs who knew Ingelise; they came to the fellowship and began to accept Jesus as Savior and be filled with the Holy Spirit. Some renounced demons and were set free spiritually. Word spread quickly about the Bronxville Fellowship meetings. One afternoon there was a knock on the door. Two girls had come to ask if the Concordia Lutheran College could come to the fellowship. Another wave of students arrived and was touched by the Holy Spirit; as a result of this, we established daily prayer meetings as the Concordia Lutheran College.

Creative Ways to Build Christian Community

Word continued to spread, and the Bronxville Fellowship was written up in a feature story by a Jewish woman reporter from the Yonkers newspaper. The paper had a large circulation, and we were visited by many in the New York area, people of all ages. This led the members of the Bronxville Fellowship to minister at a Christian Alcoholic Rehab. Many people came to the Lord there. One person at the Christian Alcoholic Rehab was delivered from a host of demons.

The work of the Bronxville Fellowship was not without cost. People in the neighborhood were wondering what I was doing, since I had originally been a Washington, DC, lawyer. My father-in-law struggled with my transition from law to ministry, even though he was a Christian. The Bronxville Fellowship differed from the traditional, formal Christian experience of my father-in-law. To alleviate tension, the Lord opened a door for me to work at a service station. The Lord touched the heart of my boss, the owner of the service station, and his entire family along with some customers who all came to Jesus.

The Bronxville Christian Fellowship conducted a retreat, what we called an "advance," for students from the University of Virginia and Dartmouth College. We took the group to Times Square where Arthur Blessitt was ministering. At Arthur Blessitt's revival, we saw many come to the Lord in a single night. Our work in New York with the Bronxville Christian Fellowship ended in 1975 when the Lord called me to Gordon- Conwell Theological Seminary to begin studying formally for the ministry in 1976.

THE BEVERLY CHRISTIAN FELLOWSHIP

I was aware that our coming to New England involved revival and not just seminary education. On arrival, we began

A Look at New Beginnings

a house meeting with Noel and Ingelise, two members of the Bronxville Christian Fellowship who had come to New England before us. The Lord led us to begin an intentional community, which we called The Beverly Christian Fellowship. This fellowship consisted of students, seminarians, and young couples. The lives of the members of the Beverly Christian Fellowship were knit together as we supported one another in various regional ministries. Some from our group went on to plant churches elsewhere. The laity of Beverly Christian Fellowship was a professionally diverse group. Some of these people went on to become psychological counselors, one is the head of an engineering firm, and another became a teacher. The members of this fellowship remain close and have been instrumental in God's continuing work in my life and that of my wife Marjean.

In addition to my work with the Beverly Christian Fellowship, God called me to accept a pastorate with a local church while I worked on my seminary studies. I also worked part-time as a chaplain at the Lynn City Hospital. My schedule was very full, and, when I graduated from Gordon-Conwell Seminary, I retained leadership of the church in Beverly and another local church nearby. I ministered at one church in the morning and then the other church in the evening.

As it all became too much to balance, I finally had to resign from all of the positions except the local church pastorate. In my time as pastor, there were many who came to the Lord. Deep down I felt there was more to do. I began fasting for revival. Edwin Orr, a well-known revivalist and professor of history at Fuller Seminary, came to New England. I was electrified by his teaching. He said that the Pentecostals believed in an individual baptism of the Holy Spirit. I imagined a whole region or nation touched by revival, just as I had studied in seminary. This vision really gripped me. I gave my life to the Lord for this purpose and began mobilizing my church for prayer. Initially, there was a great response, but I was unprepared for the spiritual warfare that followed. Conflict set in our church, which went from fast growing to a dead halt. It was very painful, as I experienced betrayal from a trusted leader. However, I could not stop my course and continued to pursue God's will.

CONCERTS OF PRAYER

I had an encounter with David Bryant of the Concerts of Prayer. From him, I learned that the practice of Concerts of Prayer dated back to the time of Jonathan Edwards and the Great Awakening. I began to lead Concerts of Prayer and conduct prayer seminars throughout New England.

In the summer of 1988, our family was away on a quiet little lake in the center of the Adirondacks. Every morning, I would have a quiet time on a floating deck on the lake. One morning, as the mist ascended from the lake, I heard the Lord say, "I am calling you to go to the church in New England. I want you to pray for revival." I was very excited and began to praise the Lord. This joy lasted for an entire day. Reality set in the next morning. "But how, Lord?" I asked. I pictured myself going around to churches and knocking on doors. The Lord didn't answer. Shortly after that, I began to attend meetings sponsored by the Evangelistic Association of New England (EANE). The Evangelistic Association of New England is now called Vision New England. There were about 100 pastors present at each EANE meeting. After several meetings, the leader stated that he was going to go somewhere else to teach. Knowing of my interest in prayer for revival, he urged me to take his position in leading.

A Look at New Beginnings

I became close to Don Gill, the President of the EANE. He said that someone needs to go around New England and see what God is doing. I volunteered. The word that the Lord had spoken to me previously was fulfilled. I began to travel throughout the region doing Concerts of Prayer and meeting with pastors. I was still, however, a pastor of a church. Finally, I was challenged by a board member. In effect, he said that my heart was no longer in the pastorate. It was true, so I resigned.

One day, as I was driving through the Maine woods, the Lord gave me another vision. I was lifted up over the region, and I looked down. I saw small campfires here and there, and people were huddling around the fires. Everyone was unaware of the existence of the other campfires around them. The Lord told me that I was to connect the campfires. I began visiting intercessors' groups and pastors' groups and built a network of prayer in New England.

I also encouraged the pastors' groups to do regional concerts of prayer. I got a grant from the Day Foundation with Steve Macchia of EANE. This grant paid for a Prayer Journey through New England. In a van, I traveled through six states accompanied by ten pastors and two intercessors. Brandt Gillespie, who provided the van, acted as the group's communication center. During the day, we met with pastors' groups, and at night we led Concerts of Prayer.

PASTORS' PRAYER SUMMIT AND INTERPRAYER

Some time later in a meeting in Oregon, I met a prayer leader named Paul Greene, who suggested that the Pastors' Prayer Summit should be brought to New England. I knew this direction was from the Lord, so I spoke with Steve

Creative Ways to Build Christian Community

Macchia about the idea. Steve agreed, and we began to have Pastors' Prayer Summits in New England.

The last ministry I was privileged to partner with and bring to New England was InterPrayer. In the early 1990s, I met an Englishman named Brian Mills, who joined me on a prayer journey around New England. I was then invited to participate in an English prayer walk from London to Berlin. I was able to participate in the leg of the prayer walk that went from Hanover to Berlin. It remains a high point in my memories. We prayer-walked between twenty to twenty-five miles a day, being led by Graham Kendrick, an intercessor and musician. Graham wrote many contemporary hymns and choruses, including "Shine, Jesus, Shine." We walked through country, forests, small towns, and cities and prayed for Germany. Part of our purpose was to pray for reconciliation between the United Kingdom and Germany in the aftermath of World War II. At night, we conducted Concerts of Prayer. We became a community made up of German, English, and American people.

One night, a former East German Communist officer fell into my arms weeping and repenting for his hatred of Americans. When we arrived in Berlin, we walked past Checkpoint Charlie. The Berlin Wall had been taken down. Rejoicing in the reconciliation that had taken place, we led 70,000 Germans in a Jesus March, which included the Mayor of Berlin. He fell at one of the Englishman's feet and repented of Germany's WWII war crimes. We passed a fallen statue of Lenin being dragged out of town in chains.

After this spiritually victorious event, I joined Brian Mills in forming a ministry called InterPrayer. InterPrayer is an international ministry of prayer to all the nations. This ministry formation led to prayer walking around the United Kingdom, Switzerland, Italy, Uganda, and Brazil. The ministry's agenda from the Lord is to reopen old wells

A Look at New Beginnings

of revival and reconciliation. Brian Mills has traveled the world with a reconciliation agenda, which has led to ongoing healing in Northern Ireland, Bosnia, and many other nations. One night, as I slept in Brian's office, I had a dream from the Lord. In the first part of the dream, I was in Norway wondering how Norwegians could stand no sun in the winter. Then the scene of the dream shifted to inner-city Boston, and I was surrounded by African-Americans. I was fearful in the dreams, but the Christians in the group stood up for me, and I was saved. Then I awoke. I asked the Lord, "What does Norway have to do with inner-city America?" The Lord responded that He was going to raise up a team of Christians to go to the nations. People would take notice because of the unity among diverse cultures.

The first journey of InterPrayer was composed of two British/American teams in the United Kingdom. The purpose of the prayer journey was to open the wells of revival and to renew covenants. One team headed south to Plymouth, England, and walked where the original pilgrims walked to board the Mayflower. When the team reached the exact point of Mayflower's departure, they prayed and seven rainbows appeared. When I heard this, I was very excited but a little jealous. Why had the Lord not sent rainbows to my team? The answer came as we departed Holy Island, a small island in the North Sea only reachable by a tidal causeway. As we drove on the causeway, I noticed a rainbow forming on the ocean, next to the causeway. As we watched, the rainbow moved toward the van. Suddenly, I felt a laser beam of rainbow light come right through the windshield and directly into my chest. I could feel the energy of the rainbow's light and gasped. I would have questioned what I saw and felt, but the other members of the team saw and felt the same thing. I fell silent and pondered this. When I returned home to Beverly, MA, I asked my prayer partner what this experience meant. He prayed that night and told me that the Lord revealed to him that this was a covenantal anointing.

This word was soon fulfilled. My friend Brian and I and another English friend were invited to a reconciliation service at what was then New Covenant Church in Boston. I had invited a young intercessor from Connecticut to join us on the platform. She went over to Dr. Ray Hammond and fell at his feet repenting for the sins of an ancestor who had been in the Ku Klux Klan and had killed a black man. That act of identificational repentance brought a breakthrough, and several hundred white pastors and intercessors came forward and asked to be prayed for by the black congregation. They received forgiveness, and the Holy Spirit was released on the assembly. After the service, everyone stayed for an hour just hugging one another. In the months that followed, I encountered people who testified how that service had changed them; something had been broken off their lives.

NEW ENGLAND CONCERTS OF PRAYER

In the past twenty years, I have interceded in prayer internationally as founder of New England Concerts of Prayer (NECP). I founded this ministry over twenty years ago to examine Scripture and the power of covenantal relationships with God that together brings spiritual revival. NECP focuses on an overview of American history, the Covenants, and the Awakenings, identifying how the Covenants and prayer shaped the United States.[1]

NECP developed through a Christian network committed to prayer. My burden for the nation grew, and, as I

1. Marks, *When New England Prays*, 5.

mentioned earlier, the Lord led me to David Bryant, founder of Concerts of Prayer, which was modeled on the vision of Jonathan Edwards. As my association with David continued, I started NECP and entered into a ministry of prayer.[2] The burden of revival and prayer for the nations was planted in me while I worked in Washington, DC, as an attorney for the Department of Housing and Urban Development. I was invited by the former Chaplain of the U.S. Senate, Dr. Richard Halverson, who was at the time a pastor at Fourth Presbyterian Church in the DC suburbs, to join in a prayer meeting that was held in his basement. It was a multi-ethnic prayer meeting, and the agenda for the meeting was for the nation's capitol. Through Dr. Halverson's mentoring in that basement prayer meeting, my understanding widened, and I realized that my prayers for New England were actually global prayers. God started opening doors to several global intercessory prayer communities.

PRAYER CONFERENCE AT THE 12TH STREET BAPTIST CHURCH IN ROXBURY, MA, IN 1990

Through the help of my friend Christy Wilson, a former missions' professor at Gordon-Conwell Seminary, I led a conference on John Eliot at the 12th Street Baptist Church in Roxbury, MA, in 1990. During the conference, the African-American members of the church community joined with me to pray for understanding of Native American issues. At the close of the conference, the entire community prayer walked through Roxbury with blacks, whites, and Latinos led by an Indian chief in full regalia. The prayer walk ended at the cemetery where John Eliot was buried.

2. Ibid., 16.

Creative Ways to Build Christian Community

The local police gave us an escort because the police commissioner feared that we might encounter hostility in the community. The movement of the Holy Spirit was so great during the prayer walk that a hush fell over the center of Roxbury. The march ended with prayer at Eliot's grave for his work among the Native American community to continue. I mention this historic event because the cultural barriers broken down by the power of prayer were evident. A cross-cultural community developed, and those involved remained in close contact in spite of the differences among them.[3]

LOU ENGLE AND THE CALL 2001

Brian Simmons, a pastor from Connecticut, was pivotal in bringing The Call to New England. The Call is the mission God gave to Lou Engle to put out a summons, particularly to youth in the United States, to return to the Lord. The Call held solemn assemblies in seven national cities. Boston was one of them. David Macadam, a pastor and gifted playwright from Concord, MA, had networked with members of the Mashemtucket reservation to write a play about the "Praying Indians." I asked David to bring the Praying Indians to The Call, to recite the Lord's Prayer in Algonquin. The Call Boston took place eleven days after September 11, 2001. The event received a terrorist threat. The members of the Indian community almost did not attend for fear of extinction. But Caring Hands, a chief, arrived with a birch bark with the Lord's Prayer written upon it in Algonquin. She found the bark in the woods while receiving a vision of reading this to thousands. Her prophetic vision became a reality that night as The Call united the Native American

3. Ibid., 83.

A Look at New Beginnings

Mashemtucket community with the will of God to ignite spiritual revival in Boston.[4]

THE WORLD REVIVAL CONFERENCE IN GUATEMALA IN 1998

Through spiritual community with Milo Siilata and Michael Malieu, I developed a deeper awareness of the Holy Spirit's guidance while at a World Revival Conference. I met Milo Siilata, who was part of a prayer team from Australia, at the World Revival Conference in Guatemala in 1998. On that journey, I was assigned to the same bus as Michael Malieu. During the Guatemalan conference, Milo related the vision of the deep sea canoe, the commuter train of the South Pacific for centuries. Citizens of the South Pacific learned to ride the winds and the currents, and Milo insisted that Christians need similarly to ride the wind of the Holy Spirit, as Jesus mentioned in the third chapter of the gospel of John.[5] I reflect on that conference and the network of believers that were instrumental in helping me catch the vision of a coming worldwide revival. This revival is being shaped by the prayers of those who covenant with God to fulfill the Great Commission to bring the lost to Jesus before his return.

CONCLUSION

As I reflect on the decades spent in intercessory prayer and prayer walking around the world, I marvel at what God has accomplished through Marjean and me since we began the Bronxville Christian Fellowship. Jesus laid out the plan of

4. Ibid., 84.
5. Ibid., 31.

Creative Ways to Build Christian Community

our Christian life and connected the dots from ministry to ministry to fulfill his great commission. The models of building Christian prayer communities set forth in this chapter resonate with my heart and soul's desire to bring souls to Jesus before his triumphant return. Each person in each ministry is precious to me as I recall the community that developed through prayer, fasting, and prayer walking. The best is yet to come: worldwide revival and the return of Jesus.

6

Summing It Up

Olga Soler

IF MINISTRY IS ONLY the work of professional clergy and is restricted to what goes on at a church service or a major Christian event, then the church is lost and doomed to implode and die in our century. Why? Because, though these things may serve God, the personal touch is often lacking in them. People think clergy pray because that's what they are paid to do. Many people are church-phobic. Large gatherings may attract people, but they cannot keep them. Happily, there is more to church and ministry than these. Ministry is what the whole priesthood of true believers everywhere does every day in the course of their faithful lives. It is what they do because they love the Lord and are called according to his purpose. It is what they are because Christ lives in them, and they are his. Real church is not an institution or a corporation. It is a loving, hospitable family that reaches out to the world the way Jesus' hands of love and healing did when he was in the world. So, if the answer is this simple, why do we need books like the one you are holding? We need them because the meaning of true ministry and church may be lost in the fray of the spiritual war that is raging for the conquest of this earth. We must keep taking it back to the biblical norm in order for all of us in the church to survive and join in the victory won by our precious Lord.

No amount of money, sophisticated projects, grand displays, or facilities with impressive or elaborate architecture will make up for the power of what God can do with a community that is functioning in the way that Christ intended it to: being continually enriched and expanded by tapping into all the gifts God has given to its members. Christ told us how to do it in his word, and the value of this plan has not diminished through the centuries. If we are to each other and to the world what he wants us to be, the harvest will soon be reaped, and we will all go home.

It all begins when we realize how truly precious real community is. In the words of Dietrich Bonheoffer, as he reflected on fellowship from a cell in a Nazi prison,

> It is easily forgotten that the fellowship of Christian brethren is a gift of grace, a gift of the Kingdom of God that at any day now may be taken from us, that the time that still separates us from utter loneliness may be brief indeed. Therefore, let him who until now has had the privilege of living a common Christian life with other Christians praise God's grace from the bottom of his heart. Let him thank God on his knees and declare: it is grace, nothing but grace that we are allowed to live in community with Christian brethren.[1]

Yes! When every job possible is automated, every materialistic need met, every gadget conceivable invented, and people have seen every special effect on film in a depersonalized futuristic utopia of science fiction, the personal touch will still be in demand. Stories told by human beings will still mean something. A letter written by hand will still

1. Bonheoffer, *Life Together*, 20.

Summing It Up

be valued. A meal cooked and shared in a hospitable home or church will still be a delight. A song sung by a voice near you or the mystery of a work of human art will still draw people in. A prayer or teaching shared person to person will still heal, edify, encourage, and inspire. The love shown by another person will still be an incomparable thing. How does one create a real community with Christ within? By taking all the gifts he gives us and helping us share them with each other and with the world.

Why do we need community? Simply put, because of Christ. He is in us, and we are one in him. This is a spiritual reality even if it is not apparent in the many expressions of Christianity. Those who truly believe are one. Again Bonheoffer speaks in this regard: "Christianity means community through Jesus Christ. . ..It means first that a Christian needs others because of Jesus Christ. It means, second, that a Christian comes to others only through Jesus Christ. It means, third, that in Jesus Christ we have been chosen from eternity, accepted in time, and united for eternity."[2]

This little book has given us some good ideas, but it is not exhaustive. Still, we touched upon some quintessential aspects of community, for example, intercession. We intercede for the world in prayer, and we see great and wonderful things because our God is real and he answers. Networking and socializing is another. Jesus went to weddings. In the gospels we see him and his disciples at many social events. He was a high-profile figure as well as up close and personal, and we should be too. Home ministry is also important, making the church less an institution and more a communal "home." In all of these, we open our hearts to the world around us, showing forth his love and healing power.

2. Ibid., 21

Creative Ways to Build Christian Community

Then there is the sharing of our gifts. Real community does not limit its members to one or two people's ways of doing things, but makes room for the infinite creativity with which the community is endowed. We minister to one another with the supernatural gifts of the Holy Spirit that are given to build us up and mature us. Everyone brings something to the table of fellowship. We trust each other in the Lord. We become intimate friends, listening to each other's cares and encouraging each other in the faith. We meet frequently to enjoy each other's fellowship, not just in a formal service where we only see the back of our brother or sister's head. We recognize that Christ is our constant companion because we recognize him in each other. We do creative things together. We take care of each other. We protect each other. We encourage each other in godliness. We love and pray for each other and for our enemies. We have fun together. We help each other when we need help. And, as a result, others cannot help but be attracted to our gatherings because what we have is not found in a mere club or bar or even in a support group. This is abundant life, the life we live together with Christ.

Is your expression of church like this? If not, then you have some work to do. In the New Testament, you will find the expression "one another" referring to how the body of Christ should behave toward each other. There are over fifty such references. It is a word study worth doing to look for these statements of "one another" or the Greek word *allelon* in the New Testament. If you can start implementing those, then you will see wonderful changes in your fellowship. In addition, you can also begin to think outside of your boxes. God is not confined to them, you know.

We hope this little book can give you some ideas about how to create and cultivate Christian community, but really God is not limited to our experiences. He can show up

Summing It Up

in a unique expression of ministry in each person in your fellowship and in every fellowship in the world. The most important thing to remember is that Christ is the sovereign head of the body, and, if you are not afraid and you listen to him, you will soon be doing things you never expected that will be effective for ministry and community.

Christ is the North Star by which we must navigate all things. To aim to become his effective community that hears the voice of the Spirit and does what he says, that functions as one in the mind of Christ, is very important. Such a community will include hospitality, intercession, instruction, physical and spiritual nourishment, creativity, networking, outreach, and social interaction. If all of these things are done in love, they are the "how" of community. Just before his crucifixion, Jesus prayed that his people would be a united and vital community. Do you remember it? This is what he said: "My prayer is not for them alone. I pray also for those who will believe in me through their message, that all of them may be one, Father, just as you are in me and I am in you. May they also be in us so that the world may believe that you have sent me" (John 17:20–22 NIV).

Our eye needs to be "single," or focused on Christ, but our heart needs to be open in love because he is our focus and he is love. Yes, there is only one way to heaven and that is him, but there are many ways to show that glorious truth to others. He is the conductor, and we are the majestic orchestra. No instrument is less important than another. Let's give Jesus the last word on community, shall we?

> As the Father has loved me, so have I loved you. Now remain in my love. If you keep my commands, you will remain in my love, just as I have kept my Father's commands and remain in his love. I have told you this so that my joy may

be in you and that your joy may be complete. My command is this: Love each other as I have loved you. Greater love has no one than this: to lay down one's life for one's friends. You are my friends if you do what I command. I no longer call you servants, because a servant does not know his master's business. Instead, I have called you friends, for everything that I learned from my Father I have made known to you. You did not choose me, but I chose you and appointed you so that you might go and bear fruit—fruit that will last—and so that whatever you ask in my name the Father will give you. This is my command: Love each other. (John 15:9–17 NIV)

Contributors

Jeanne DeFazio is a former actress of Spanish/ Italian descent, straight out of Hollywood, who left the glitz and glamour of a career of make-believe, playing supporting parts in movies and television series, to disappear into a life of service to the marginalized in the drama of real life. Jeanne became a teacher of second-language-learner children in the barrios of San Diego. A woman of great faith, intelligence, and energy, she responded to God's calling, pursuing seminary education at Gordon-Conwell Theological Seminary, and, after graduation, returning as an Athanasian Teaching Scholar at its multicultural Boston Center for Urban Ministerial Education (CUME), which serves the often unnoticed but thriving ethnic churches. (Dr. William David Spencer, "Introduction," *How to Have an Attitude of Gratitude on the Night Shift*, Soltice Press, Oakland, 2010).

Teresa Two Feathers Flowers, who hails from Amarillo, Texas, is of Cherokee and Lebanese/Dutch descent, and is generally in public as silent as the desert on a starry night. Two Feathers speaks through her others-oriented actions and the economy of her poems. Whatever practical needs to be done, she does it. Currently, she is the elder who serves with the deacons of Pilgrim Church, a storefront mission church in the small city of Beverly, Massachusetts. Many Sundays, Two Feathers volunteers to cook a meal free to the public and consequently feeds

Contributors

a small army composed of anyone who drops in, using a budget (mainly provided by her) about the size of a one-family trip to McDonald's. Think of a cook on a cattle drive, gently soothing the calves, thoroughly nourishing the cowhands on a larder of next to nothing, devoutly communing with God on the high plains, and steadily persevering through rain and wind and snow and hail, ever calm, pleasant, constant, capable, and totally reliable. (Dr. William David Spencer, "Introduction," *How to Have an Attitude of Gratitude on the Night Shift*. Soltice Press, Oakland, 2010).

Jeff Marks is a graduate of Dartmouth College, Dickinson Law School, and Gordon-Conwell Theological Seminary. God called Jeff out of a career as an attorney at the U.S. Department of Housing and Urban Development into full-time ministry with the Fellowship Foundation under the leadership of Dr. Richard Halverson. A mobilizer and prayer leader for more than 25 years, Jeff has been the director of New England Concerts of Prayer (NECP) since 1990 and is a member of the National Prayer Committee. Jeff is the author of *When New England Prays: America's Covenant With God,* which focuses on God's covenants with America, Israel, and the nations.

Olga Soler is director/writer and performer for Estuary Ministries, a Christ-centered performing arts ministry dealing with biblical themes, inner healing, abuse, and addictive problems. The art forms used include drama, dance, storytelling, mime, comedy, graphic arts, writing, film, and song. Olga attended the High School of Performing Arts ("Fame"), the Lee Strasberg Theater Institute, and the Herbert Berghof Studios, in New York City. She has performed widely at conferences, churches, prisons, coffee houses, support groups, youth groups, and retreats and has even performed on the streets, at secular colleges, and in worship services across the United States and the United Kingdom. She holds degrees in education and communications with equivalent studies in theology and psychology. She studied for two years at Gordon Conwell Theological Seminary. She has designed and conducted the workshops "Dance Alive" and "Trauma Drama" at many Christian Recovery conferences. She wrote the curriculum for and conducted Discovery Groups for addicts at the Boston Rescue Mission, using the arts to help them process aspects of their recovery. She also conducts workshops for Christian drama and dance in many churches of all denominations. Using Paulo Freire's "pedagogy of the oppressed," she wrote a script for the "Mosaics" group of parents helping their children who were victims of sexual abuse through the courts system and assisted them in filming the script for a documentary. She performed and coauthored scripts for four years with the "Team" Christian Ministry in Massachusetts and conducted eight full-scale multimedia presentations out of the Rio Ondo Arts Place in Woburn, MA, including "Voice of the Martyrs," "Techno Easter," and "Clean Comedy Night." She has directed and choreographed entire productions at universities and colleges, including "A Man for All Seasons," "Jane Eyre," "Amal and the Night Visitors," and (by permission of the author) Calvin Miller's "The Singer." She wrote and illustrated the book *Epistle to the Magadalenes* and has conducted retreats for women using the book accompanied by dramatic presentation. She is the author of many other books and assorted screenplays. She is the proud mother of three wonderful children

Contributors

Cielo, Reva, and Ransom. She lives in Massachusetts with her husband Chris and her Japanese Chin (dog), Kiji.

William David Spencer is Ranked Adjunct Full Professor of Theology and the Arts at Gordon-Conwell Theological Seminary, Director of the Athanasian Teaching Scholars Program, Co-director of the Africanus Guild PhD Support Program, Co-editor of *Africanus Journal* (CUME), Editor of *Priscilla Papers* (Christians for Biblical Equality), Co-producer of the House of Prisca and Aquila Series (Wipf and Stock, Publishers), and Founding Pastor of Encouragement, Pilgrim Church, Beverly, MA. He is the author of twelve books and over 200 articles, poems, stories, editorials, and book reviews. He is married to Aída Besançon Spencer.

Cathy Squires is a University of California, Berkeley, and Holy Names University graduate in psychology and counseling psychology. She spent her adult years focusing on personal healing and spiritual growth as well as on early childhood education and early childhood mental health. To her, children have a special way of opening our eyes to the extraordinary with the ordinary. She was born in India to Chinese parents and grew up in Pakistan and Hong Kong. She is mother to four children (biological and adopted) and grandmother to ten (living and departed). She facilitates classes for Life Skills International and enjoys individual Spiritual Direction. She has plans to develop a small urban retreat home in West Sacramento, California, where she resides with her husband Bill.

Bibliography

Bonhoeffer, Dietrich. *Life Together*. New York, NY: Harper and Row, 1954.

British & Foreign Bible Society. "The Masoretes and the Punctuation of Biblical Hebrew." (May 2, 2002). Online: http://boulders2bits.com/wordpress/wp-content/uploads/Masoretes.pdf.

DeFazio, Jeanne and Teresa Flowers. *How to Have an Attitude of Gratitude on the Night Shift*. Oakland, CA: Solstice, 2011.

Freeman, James M., and Harold J. Chadwick. *The New Manners and Customs of the Bible*. Rev. ed. Alachua, FL: Bridge-Logos, 1998.

Haidt, Jonathan. *The Righteous Mind: Why Good People Are Divided by Politics and Religion*. New York, NY: Pantheon, 2012.

Lah, Kyung. "Tokyo Man Marries Video Game Character." (December 17, 2009). Cited 2 January 2010. Online: http://www.cnn.com/2009/WORLD/asiapcf/12/16/japan.virtual.wedding/index.html.

Marks, Jeff. *When New England Prays: America's Covenant With God*. Self publication. Beverly, Mass.: 2008.

Mooney, Chris. "Your Brain on Politics: The Cognitive Neuroscience of Liberals and Conservatives." *Discover Magazine*, (September 27, 2011).

Navarro, Nicole. "Man Marries Video Game Character." Cited February 12, 2013. Online: http://indieregister.com/2009/12/23/man-marries-video-game-character/.

Newman Jr., Barclay M. *A Concise Greek-English Dictionary of the New Testament*. Stuttgart, Germany: Deutsche Bibelgesellschaft/United Bible Societies, 1993.

Phillips, John. "California Dreamin.'" Santa Monica, CA: Universal Music Publishing Group, 1978.

Snell, Joe. "Impacts of Robotic Sex." Cited in *Love and Sex with Robots: The Evolution of Human-Robot Relationships*, by David Levy. New York: HarperCollins, 2007.

Bibliography

Time Video, "Californians Bring Passion to Jerusalem's Old City." Cited September 11, 2012. Online: http://www.time.com/time/video/player/0,32068,75560426001_1977063,00.html.

Viola, Frank and George Barna. *Pagan Christianity*. Carroll Stream, IL: Tyndale, 2008.

Walker, Deborah Gardner. "Teresa Flowers: Healing Pain with Good Cooking." *Beverly Citizen* (August 11, 2011). Cited February 9, 2013. Online: http://www.wickedlocal.com/beverly/newsnow/x919524308/Teresa-Flowers-Healing-pain-with-good-cooking#ixzz1uNs4a5q3.